HIJAB

The Islamic Commandments of Hijab

Dr. Mohammed Ismail Memon Madani

English Translation

Dr. Mohammed Sadiq

Islamic Book Service

HIJAB

Dr. Mohammed Ismail Memon Madani

ISBN 81-7231-342-X

Reprint Edition : 2007

Published by *Abdul Naeem* for

Islamic Book Service

2872-74, Kucha Chelan, Darya Ganj
New Delhi 110 002 (INDIA)
Ph.: 011-23253514, 23286551, 23244556, 23247899
Fax: 011-23277913 **E-mail:** islamic@eth.net
Website: www.islamic-india.com

Our Associates:

Al-Munna Book Shop Ltd., (U.A.E.)
Sharjah *Tel.:* 06-561-5483, 06-561-4650 **Dubai** *Tel.:* 04-352-9294
Azhar Academy Ltd., London (United Kingdom)
Tel.: 020 8911 9797
I.B. Publisher Inc., New York (U.S.A.)
Tel.: 91-73328008, 6312540909
Husami Book Depot (Hyderabad)
Tel.: 040-6680-6285

Printed at Islamic@eth.net

TABLE OF CONTENTS

ACKNOWLEDGEMENTS i

TRANSLATOR'S NOTE iii

INTRODUCTION v

CHAPTER ONE 1

EVIDENCE FROM THE HOLY QUR'ĀN 1
- THE VERSE OF HIJĀB 1
- CIRCUMSTANCES SURROUNDING THE REVELATION OF THE ABOVE VERSE 5
- COMMANDMENT FOR WOMEN TO STAY HOME 7
- BURQA' OR JALBĀB 14
  - WHAT IS JALBĀB 16
  - HOW TO WRAP THE SHEET AROUND 18
- THE COMMANDMENT FOR PROTECTING GAZE AND HIDING ADORNMENT 21
  - LOWERING THE EYES (GHADD AL-BASAR) 22
  - GUARDING THE MODESTY (PRIVATE PARTS) 23
  - CONCEALING THE BEAUTY AND ORNAMENTS 24
  - CONCEALING THE SOUND 27
- A DANGEROUS MISUNDERSTANDING 29
- SEEKING PERMISSION BEFORE ENTERING A HOUSE 32
- FOR ELDERLY WOMEN 33
- SUMMARY 34

CHAPTER TWO 36

EVIDENCE FROM AHĀDĪTH 36
- THE HIJĀB OF THE FEMALE COMPANIONS OF THE PROPHET 36
  - OBSERVANCE OF HIJĀB EVEN IN DISTRESS 37
  - OBSERVING HIJĀB WHILE MAKING BAI'AH 39
- OBSERVING HIJĀB IN FRONT OF THE COMPANIONS OF THE PROPHET 40

HIJĀB FOR WOMEN SERVANTS ... 43
OBSERVING HIJĀB DURING MEDICAL TREATMENT ... 44
TO UNCOVER SATR FOR MEDICAL TREATMENT ... 45
HIJĀB UNDER IHRĀM ... 46
HIJĀB WITH IN-LAWS ... 47
MODESTY (HAYĀ) AND HONOUR ... 48
TO GO OUT WITHOUT NECESSITY ... 52
OFFERING SALĀT AT HOME ... 54
PARTICIPATION IN JIHĀD ... 56
ETIQUETTES OF EMERGING FROM HOME ... 57
THE USE OF PERFUME AND ORNAMENTS ... 57
EMERGING FROM HOME WITHOUT HUSBAND'S PERMISSION ... 58
TRAVELLING ALONE ... 59
WALKING ON THE STREET ... 60
GUARDING THE EYES ... 61
WILLFULLY GOING TO A PLACE WHERE HIJĀB IS NOT BEING OBSERVED ... 63
BEING ALONE WITH GHAIR-MAHRAM MAN ... 64
BATHING IN PUBLIC SHOWERS ... 66
LOOKING AT MEN ... 68
ADOPTING THE WAYS OF THE OPPOSITE SEX ... 69
COMMANDMENTS ABOUT DRESS ... 70
PROHIBITION OF NUDITY AND REQUIREMENT OF SATR ... 71
CLOTHING ... 73
TIGHT AND SEE THROUGH CLOTHES ... 74
TOUCHING GHAIR-MAHRAM WOMEN ... 76
DESCRIBING OTHER WOMEN'S ATTRIBUTES TO HUSBAND ... 77
WEARING NOISY ORNAMENTS ... 78
ENTERING SOMEBODY'S HOUSE WITH PERMISSION ... 79

CHAPTER THREE ... 82

THE ISLAMIC SYSTEM FOR THE PREVENTION OF OBSCENITIES ... 82
CUTTING OFF THE MEANS - THE GOLDEN PRINCIPLE OF PREVENTING CRIMES ... 83
THE HISTORY OF THE COMMANDMENTS OF HIJĀB ... 87
THE DIFFERENCE BETWEEN HIJĀB AND SATR ... 89

THE CATEGORIES OF SHARA'Ī HIJĀB AND THEIR COMMANDMENTS 91
FIRST CATEGORY OF HIJĀB - REMAINING IN HOME 92
SECOND CATEGORY OF HIJĀB - BY BURQA' 95

CHAPTER FOUR 100

THE ANCIENT AGE OF JĀHILĪYAH AND PRESENT DAY JĀHILĪYAH 100
SEVERAL EXAMPLES OF INDECENCY IN THE PRESENT DAY JĀHILĪYAH 101
A SUMMARY OF THE DETAILS OF HIJĀB AND THE INTENTIONS OF SHARĪ'AH 107
A COMPARISON BETWEEN THE WOMEN OF THE EAST AND THE WEST 108
A MOMENT OF THOUGHT 113

GLOSSARY 120

ACKNOWLEDGEMENTS

First and foremost, I thank Allah (s.w.t.) for His Mercy and Guidance in this work. I also wish to thank Dr. Mohammed Ismail Memon Madani for his inspiration and encouragement in translating this book. He was also kind enough to review the entire book and suggest valuable changes before it was published. I would also like to thank Maulānā Ibrāhīm Memon and Brother M. A. Qazi for their assistance in correcting the translation of various terms and proper nouns. I am thankful as well to Mrs. Noman for helping me in the translation of chapter four of this book and all the brothers and sisters who read the manuscript and suggested vaulable changes. Last but not least, I would like to thank my family, especially my sons Irfan and Javaid Tawheed who have assisted me every step of the way in this work. May Allah be pleased with them.

Mohammed Sadiq

TRANSLATOR'S NOTE

All Praise be to Allah; we praise and seek Guidance from Him; we have Faith in Him and we place our trust in Him. We seek the Protection of Allah from the evil of our *Nafs* and our deeds. May He shower *Salāt* and *Salām* on our beloved Prophet Muhammad (s.a.w.) and on his family and his Companions.

I have made every attempt to use simple and contemporary English in the translation of this book. However, there were many times where a simple English word could not be found to convey the meaning and, therefore, either the original word in Urdu or Arabic was retained with a footnote explaining its meaning, or a word from old English was substituted.

I also edited the book leaving out some parts from the original text which were repetitious. These editorial changes were reviewed and approved by the author of the original book, Dr. Mohammed Ismail Memon Madani.

My main objective in translating this book was to provide my Muslim brothers and sisters and our youth living in North America and other Western countries with an authentic peace of work in the English language on the necessity of Hijāb so that they could read it themselves and appreciate the wisdom behind these golden Commandments of Islam.

May Allah accept this work and make it useful for those who truly desire to learn and practice Islam in their lives.

Dr. Mohammed Sadiq
Edmonton, Alberta, Canada
Ramadhan 18, 1414 H
March 1, 1994

INTRODUCTION

There are many issues where there have not been any differences of opinion among the Muslim *Ummah* since the beginning of Islam. In fact, there has been an almost complete consensus on these issues. But, these are the days of 'reform'. 'Freedom from old traditions' seems to have become the motto. Attempts are being made to approve and accept as lawful everything that was forbidden in Islam. Many consented matters are being presented as controversial. One such issue is that of *Hijāb* [1]. One hears claims from everywhere that there is no Commandment in Islam about *Hijāb*. Some present inaccurate translations of the Holy Verses in this regard. Others bring forth uncommon interpretations of the Qur'ānic Verses about *Hijāb*. Still others refute the Ahādīth in this respect.

In western countries non-Islamic ideologies are more prevalent than Islamic education. The literature about Islam found in these countries has been written mostly by Christians and Jews, or by those so-called Muslims who have been heavily influenced by western education, or have obtained degrees in Islamic Education under the training of Jews and Christians. They, therefore, view the holy Qur'ān and Ahādīth of the Prophet (s.a.w.) through their coloured glasses. As a result, they themselves go astray and lead others on the wrong path as well. Doubts are being created about the Commandments of *Hijāb* also.

---

[1] *Hijāb* literally means screen, curtain, partition, and concealment. As a verb, it means to conceal oneself or hide from the view. In Islamic *Sharī'ah*, the word means to cover, conceal or hide oneself from the view of *Ghair-Mahram*.

Hijāb, with its established limits, is a Divine Law and Guidance based on the Holy Qur'ān and the Traditions (Ahādīth) of Prophet Muhammad (s.a.w.), the interpretations of these by the Islamic jurists as well as on the practices of our pious predecessors. It is on these bases that it has been practiced continuously at all times by the Muslim *Ummah*. It is not something fictitious that was contrived by people and given the status of Islamic Law in Muslim societies based on cultural practices. Such is not the case, nor is it befitting to expect from a comprehensive, complete and protected Divine Constitution of Islam that has no room for any modifications. But, for sometime now, people are going to extremes in its practices and beliefs. Consequently, doubts have been raised in people's minds about the legal status and the basic truth about the *Hijāb*, and it has become the target of questions and doubts.

Under the influence of western civilization, the practice of women going about without *Hijāb* has resulted in reactionary and extreme points of views about it. This has caused further doubts about its principles and its legal limits. On the one hand, the legal limits of *Hijāb* are claimed to be the results of conservatism of Islamic scholars and, instead of simply choosing not to observe *Hijāb* for oneself, people are made to believe that bringing women out in the open is the need of the day as well as the objective of the Divine Law. On the other hand, pointing out the legitimate flexibility in the Divine Law about *Hijāb* is considered heresy. This has gone on to the point where the traditional and cultural limits imposed on women are also being incorporated in the Divine Law.

It is, therefore, necessary to present the true teachings of the holy Qur'ān and the Ahādīth on this matter. May Allah give us the true understanding of the Divine Law and the courage to practice it.

In the end, I would like to thank my dear sons Mohammed Mansoor and Mohammed Ibrāhīm, who truly proved to be my hands and arms in writing this book. I am also thankful to my dear friend Maulānā Mohammed Abdul Moez who reviewed the transcript and suggested vaulable changes which have made the book better organized and more beneficial. May Allah enrich their knowledge and accept them in the service of His Dīn, and bless them with success of this world and of the world Hereafter.

NOTE: These days the word *Hijāb* is often translated in English as Head Scarf, which is not in accordance with its meaning and intent in the Holy Qur'ān and Ahādīth. It is, therefore, misleading. The correct translation is 'Something that covers and conceals completely'.

Dr. Mohammed Ismail Memon Madani
Servant, Darul-Uloom Al-Madania
182 Sobieski Street
Buffalo, N.Y., U.S.A.
Zilqadah 26, 1410 H
June 20, 1990

TRANSLITERATION OF ARABIC WORDS AND NAMES

The following table shows the system which has been followed in transliterating the letters of the Arabic Alphabets.

ا	= Alif	= a		ط	= Tā	= t
	(long vowel)	ā		ظ	= Zā	= z
ب	= Bā	= b		ع	= ‘Ayn	= ‘
ت	= Tā	= t		غ	= Ghayn	= gh
ث	= Thā	= th		ف	= Fā	= f
ج	= Jīm	= j		ق	= Qāf	= q
ح	= Hā	= h		ك	= Kāf	= k
خ	= Khā	= kh		ل	= Lām	= l
د	= Dāl	= d		م	= Mīm	= m
ذ	= Dhāl	= dh		ن	= Nūn	= n
ر	= Rā	= r		ه	= Hā	= h
ز	= Zā	= z		و	= Wāw	= w
س	= Sīn	= s			(long vowel)	= ū
ش	= Shīn	= sh		ي	= Yā	= y
ص	= Sād	= s			(long wovel)	= ī
ض	= Dād	= d		ء	= Hamzah	= ’

Short vowels:
- ´ (fathah) = a
- ˏ (kasrah) = i
- ʼ (dammah) = u

CHAPTER ONE

EVIDENCE FROM THE HOLY QUR'ĀN

The rules and regulations governing the relationship and socialization between men and women are those basics in any human civilization which, when violated, result in the destruction of the entire society. This may be readily witnessed in various times in the history of human civilization. Hence, Allah has spoken in the Holy Qur'ān in detail on this topic providing clear boundaries. For example, men and women have been asked to lower their gazes; women have been asked not to engage in sweet talk with men; and the Companions of the Prophet (s.a.w.) were asked to talk to the Wives of the Prophet from behind a curtain if they needed to ask anything from them.

THE VERSE OF *HIJĀB*

The scholars of the Holy Qur'ān agree that the Commandment regarding *Hijāb* for women was revealed in the following Verse of *Sūrah Ahzāb*, which is why this Verse is also known as the Verse of *Hijāb*.

1. يَٰٓأَيُّهَا ٱلَّذِينَ ءَامَنُوا۟ لَا تَدْخُلُوا۟ بُيُوتَ ٱلنَّبِىِّ إِلَّآ أَن
يُؤْذَنَ لَكُمْ إِلَىٰ طَعَامٍ غَيْرَ نَٰظِرِينَ إِنَىٰهُ وَلَٰكِنْ إِذَا دُعِيتُمْ
فَٱدْخُلُوا۟ فَإِذَا طَعِمْتُمْ فَٱنتَشِرُوا۟ وَلَا مُسْتَـْٔنِسِينَ لِحَدِيثٍ إِنَّ
ذَٰلِكُمْ كَانَ يُؤْذِى ٱلنَّبِىَّ فَيَسْتَحْىِۦ مِنكُمْ وَٱللَّهُ لَا
يَسْتَحْىِۦ مِنَ ٱلْحَقِّ وَإِذَا سَأَلْتُمُوهُنَّ مَتَٰعًا فَسْـَٔلُوهُنَّ مِن
وَرَآءِ حِجَابٍ ذَٰلِكُمْ أَطْهَرُ لِقُلُوبِكُمْ وَقُلُوبِهِنَّ وَمَا كَانَ
لَكُمْ أَن تُؤْذُوا۟ رَسُولَ ٱللَّهِ وَلَآ أَن تَنكِحُوٓا۟ أَزْوَٰجَهُۥ
مِنۢ بَعْدِهِۦٓ أَبَدًا إِنَّ ذَٰلِكُمْ كَانَ عِندَ ٱللَّهِ عَظِيمًا (الأحزاب:٥٣)

> O you who Believe! Enter not the Prophet's houses until permission is given to you for a meal, (and then) not (so early as) to wait for its preparation; but when you are invited, enter; and when you have taken your meal, disperse without seeking vain talk. Such (behaviour) annoys the Prophet; he is ashamed to dismiss you, but Allah is not ashamed (to tell you) the truth. And when you ask (his Wives) for anything you want, ask them from behind a screen (*Hijāb*); that makes for greater purity for your hearts and for theirs. Nor is it right for you that you should annoy Allah's Messenger, or that you should marry his widows after him at any time. Truly such a thing is in Allah's Sight an enormity. (*Sūrah Ahzāb*, v. 53)

In the above Verse, we find some etiquettes and Commandments of the Islamic way of life pertaining to:

1. Invitations for meals and the conduct of guests,
2. *Hijāb* for women, and
3. Marriage with the Wives of the Prophet (s.a.w.) after his demise.

Since #1 and #3 above are not part of our topic, I will present the details of #2.

In this Verse of *Sūrah Ahzāb*, *Hijāb* was mandated for women. Women were not required to observe *Hijāb* before the revelation of this Verse.

There is consensus among the scholars of the Holy Qur'ān that although the Wives of the Prophet (s.a.w.) were particularly addressed in this Verse, the Commandment is meant for all women. The same style of providing Guidance is found in many other places in the Holy Qur'ān. For example, Allah says in *Sūrah Talāq*:

يَاأَيُّهَاالنَّبِيُّ إِذَا طَلَّقْتُمُ النِّسَاءَ فَطَلِّقُوهُنَّ لِعِدَّتِهِنَّ وَأَحْصُوا الْعِدَّةَ (الطلاق:١)

O Prophet (s.a.w.), when you do divorce women, divorce them at their prescribed periods. (*Sūrah Talāq*, v. 1)

Clearly, not divorcing women in their prescribed periods (*'Iddat*) and waiting until they are clean, was not meant only for the Prophet (s.a.w.) and his Wives, but all Muslim men and women are bound by this Divine Law. Similarly, in the above Verse of *Sūrah Ahzāb*, although the address is specific to the Wives of the Prophet (s.a.w.), the Commandment is meant for all Muslim women. The biggest proof of this is the reason Allah (s.w.t.) stated for this Command in this Verse - ذالكم أطهرلقلوبكم وقلوبهن "...that makes for greater purity for your hearts and for theirs." This clearly means that immodesty (going without *Hijāb*) breeds filth and indecency in hearts. Undoubtedly, the common Muslim men and women are more in need of protecting themselves from this filth and indecency since they are more liable to engage in such sinful activities.

It is also noteworthy here that the women, who have been addressed in this Verse of *Hijāb*, were the Wives of the Prophet (s.a.w.) for whom Allah Himself took the responsibility to ensure the purity and cleanliness of their hearts. This has been mentioned in the same Sūrah.

إِنَّمَا يُرِيدُ اللهُ لِيُذْهِبَ عَنكُمُ الرِّجْسَ أَهْلَ الْبَيْتِ وَيُطَهِّرَكُمْ تَطْهِيرًا ۝ (الأحزاب:٣٣)

> ....(Allah wishes) to remove all abomination from you and your family members, and to make you pure and spotless. (*Sūrah Ahzāb*, v. 33)

On the other hand, the men were those respectable Companions of the Prophet (s.a.w.), many of whom were ahead of the angels in their status. When such pious people of the earlier days of Islam were bound by the Commandments of *Hijāb*, the people of later ages would be even more in need of them since the impulsiveness, egocentricity, and sexual freedom will continuously increase as the Day of Judgement comes closer. Who among us can claim that our self-control is better than that of the respectable Companions of the Prophet; that our women are more pious than the Wives of the Prophet (s.a.w.); and that there is no danger of corruption today in men and women mixing freely with each other.

In the interpretation of this Verse, Hāfiz Ibn Kathīr writes:

> Muslims were forbidden from entering the houses of the Prophet (s.a.w.) as they used to enter each other's houses without permission in the days before Islam. Allah chose modesty and honour for this *Ummah* and commanded them to observe *Hijāb*. Undoubtedly, this Commandment is in respect and honour of this *Ummah*. (*Tafsīr Ibn Kathīr*)

'Allāmah Ibn 'Arabī writes in his interpretation:

> Although the three Commandments in this Verse, i.e., entering the house of the Prophet (s.a.w.) after permission, not engaging in idle talk after the meal, and observing *Hijāb* between men and the Wives of the Prophet (s.a.w.), were revealed

specifically for the houses of the Prophet and his Wives, these are binding for all Muslims as we are required to follow the guidance and the tradition of the Prophet (s.a.w.). Unless, of course, if Allah Himself specifies that a particular rule is meant only for the Prophet (s.a.w.) and the *Ummah* is not subjected to it, which is not the case here. (*Ahkām-ul-Qur'ān*, vol. 5, p. 342)

Imām Qurtubī writes:

This Verse provides the permission to ask, from behind a screen (*Hijāb*), the Wives of the Prophet (s.a.w.) for any necessary thing, including any matters of religion. And, all Muslim women would be bound by the same rule. Besides this Verse, other principles of the Islamic doctrine also tell us that a woman (for her honour) deserves to be hidden - her body as well as her voice. (*Tafsīr-e-Qurtubī*, vol. 14, p. 227)

CIRCUMSTANCES SURROUNDING THE REVELATION OF THE ABOVE VERSE

A number of circumstances have been stated surrounding the Revelation of the above Verse. These are not contradictory. It is likely that all those circumstances together resulted in this Revelation. Ibn Abī Hātim narrated from Salman Bin Arqam, that the first part of the Verse, dealing with the etiquettes of invitations for meal, was revealed about those unruly people who showed up uninvited at meal times and waited until the meal was served.

Imām 'Abd Bin Hamīd has narrated from Anas (r.a.) that these people used to wait for the meal time and then went to the house of the Prophet (s.a.w.) and sat talking among themselves until the meal was served so that they could join in. The first two Verses were revealed to guide such people. These types of incidents occurred before the Commandments about *Hijāb* were revealed when men used to go freely into the houses of other people and their private quarters.

There are two narrations by Imām Bukhārī regarding the circumstances surrounding the Revelation of the Commandments about *Hijāb*.

One has been narrated by Anas (r.a.) that 'Umar Bin Khattāb (r.a.) said to the Prophet (s.a.w.): "O Prophet of Allah!, you receive all kinds of people at your home - good and bad; it would be better if you ask your Wives to observe *Hijāb*." Accordingly, this Verse of *Hijāb* was revealed.

There is a narration both in Bukhārī and Muslim where 'Umar Farūq (r.a.) had said: My Lord agreed with me in three things: 1. I said, "O Allah's Apostle! I wish we took the station of Prophet Ibrāhīm as our praying place (for some of our prayers)"; so came the Divine Inspiration: وَاتَّخِذُوا مِنْ مَقَامِ إِبْرَاهِيمَ مُصَلًّى "And take you (people) the station of Prophet Ibrāhīm as a place of prayer." (2:125) 2. And as regards the (Verse of) the veiling of women, I said, "O Allah's Apostle! I wish you ordered your Wives to cover themselves from the men because both the good and bad ones talk to them"; so the Verse of *Hijāb* for women was revealed. 3. Once the Wives of the Prophet (s.a.w.) became envious of each other (for the attention he gave to one of them) and banded together against him, and I said to them, "It may be if he [the Prophet (s.a.w.)] divorced you (all) that his Lord (Allah) will give him, instead of you, Wives better than you"; so a Verse was revealed in exactly the same words.

There is another narration from Anas (r.a.) in Bukhārī: Narrated Anas Bin Malik: .....I knew about the Order of *Al-Hijāb* (veiling of ladies) more than any other person when it was revealed. It was revealed for the first time when Allah's Apostle (s.a.w.) had consummated his marriage with Zainab Bint Jahsh. When the day dawned, the Prophet was a bridegroom and he invited the people to a banquet; so they came, ate, and then left, all except a few who remained with the Prophet for a long time. The Prophet got up and went out, and I too went out with him so that those people might leave too. The Prophet proceeded and so did I till he came to the threshold of 'Āishah's dwelling place. Then thinking that those people might have left, he returned and so did I along with him and behold, they were still sitting and had not gone. So the Prophet again walked away and I walked along with him. When we reached the threshold of 'Āishah's dwelling place he thought that they had left, and so he returned and I too returned along with him and found those people had left. Then the Verse of *Hijāb* was revealed يٰأَيُّهَا الَّذِيْنَ آمَنُوْا لَا تَدْخُلُوْا بُيُوْتَ النَّبِيِّ .... (which he recited to me), and drew a curtain between me and him.

COMMANDMENT FOR WOMEN TO STAY HOME

To protect the chastity of women and to maintain the moral character of a society, the most important factor is to minimize free contact between men and women. The best way to ensure this is for women not to leave their homes unnecessarily. Their excessive outings and coming in contact with (*Ghair-Mahram*)[2] men result in severe temptations, which is clearly evident in past and present ignorant societies. This is why the Holy Qur'ān specifically commanded women to stay in their homes. Allah says in *Sūrah Ahzāb*, Verses 32-33:

---

[2] Opposite of *Mahram* (i.e., a man with whom marriage is permissible and, therefore, women must observe *Hijāb* in front of them.)

2. يَٰنِسَآءَ ٱلنَّبِيِّ لَسۡتُنَّ كَأَحَدٖ مِّنَ ٱلنِّسَآءِ إِنِ ٱتَّقَيۡتُنَّۚ فَلَا تَخۡضَعۡنَ بِٱلۡقَوۡلِ
فَيَطۡمَعَ ٱلَّذِي فِي قَلۡبِهِۦ مَرَضٞ وَقُلۡنَ قَوۡلٗا مَّعۡرُوفٗا ٣٢ وَقَرۡنَ
فِي بُيُوتِكُنَّ وَلَا تَبَرَّجۡنَ تَبَرُّجَ ٱلۡجَٰهِلِيَّةِ ٱلۡأُولَىٰۖ وَأَقِمۡنَ
ٱلصَّلَوٰةَ وَءَاتِينَ ٱلزَّكَوٰةَ وَأَطِعۡنَ ٱللَّهَ وَرَسُولَهُۥٓۚ إِنَّمَا
يُرِيدُ ٱللَّهُ لِيُذۡهِبَ عَنكُمُ ٱلرِّجۡسَ أَهۡلَ ٱلۡبَيۡتِ وَيُطَهِّرَكُمۡ
تَطۡهِيرٗا (الأحزاب:٣٣-٣٢)

> O Consorts of the Prophet! You are not like any of the (other) women; if you do fear (Allah), be not too complaisant of speech, lest one in whose heart is a disease should be moved with desire; but speak you a speech (that is) just. And stay quietly in your houses, and make not a dazzling display, like that of the former Times of Ignorance; and establish regular Prayer and give regular charity (*Zakāt*); and obey Allah and His Messenger. And Allah only wishes to remove all abomination from you, you Members of the Family, and to make you pure and spotless. (*Sūrah Ahzāb*, v. 32-33)

Two important Commandments become clear from the above Verses.

First, that women should not talk to (*Ghair-Mahram*) men unnecessarily or in a soft and sweet tone of voice, but rather in a straight forward and honourable manner, so that no one will misinterpret them or have any bad thoughts about them.

Imām Qurtubī writes in the interpretation of this Verse:

> Allah has commanded Muslim women to talk in a straight forward and concise manner with (*Ghair-Mahram*) men. The tone of their voice

should be devoid of softness and sweetness unlike the street women and uncivilized women of olden days who used to sweet talk men. A woman should be very careful while talking to (*Ghair-Mahram*) men even if they are members of her in-laws. She should speak in a firm voice without being loud. (*Qurtubī*, vol. 14, pp. 177-78)

Muftī Muhammad Shafī' writes in his interpretation:

فَلَا تَخْضَعْنَ بِالْقَوْلِ means that even when it becomes necessary to talk to the (*Ghair-Mahram*) men, a woman should avoid the soft and attractive tone of voice which is part of her nature. What this means is that she should not speak in a way that might charm or attract the listener. As Allah said: فَيَطْمَعَ الَّذِيْ فِيْ قَلْبِهِ مَرَضٌ "...be not too complaisant of speech, lest one in whose heart is a disease should be moved with desire." *Disease* here refers to hypocrisy (*Nifāq*), total or partial. The true hypocrite (*Munāfiq*) would indeed be expected to behave in such a manner, but some times one, who is otherwise a true believer, may also have an inclination towards the forbidden (*Harām*) which is also part of hypocrisy. A person, who has true Faith, can never be inclined towards the forbidden (*Harām*).

The main objective of this first part of the Commandment is for women to acquire such a state of *Hijāb* and an avoidance of (*Ghair-Mahram*) men that those of weak faith may not have any hope, or greed of any favours, from them. After this Verse was revealed, some of the Wives of the Prophet (s.a.w.) used to cover their mouth with their hands to hide their natural voice while talking to strangers. 'Amer Bin 'Ās narrated from the Prophet (s.a.w.):

أن النبي صلى الله عليه وسلم نهى أن تكلم النساء إلا بإذن أزواجهن (الطبراني)

Indeed the Prophet (s.a.w.) prohibited women to talk (to *Ghair-Mahram* men) without the permission of their husbands. (*Tabrānī*)

The second important part of this Commandment states that the best way for women to observe *Hijāb* is to stay in their homes and not to come out without a valid necessity. Observing *Hijāb* in this manner is known as *Hijāb Bil Buyūt* (observing *Hijāb* by way of staying home).

Also apparent from this Verse, is that women are created in a way that they can be contented and at peace only by staying within their houses, occupying themselves with home and family matters. The welfare and prosperity of the society also depends on this. A woman's physical nature is not well suited for working outside the home like men to earn a living, and to face all the severe hardships associated with it, which only men have been equipped to deal with. This is why, in Islam, women have not been made responsible to earn a living. Her parents and brothers carry the responsibility to meet her material needs before her wedding, which is passed on to her husband after her marriage. This clearly shows how often Islam wants women to come out of their homes.

Another part of this Verse, "...and make not a dazzling display, like that of the former Times of Ignorance...", tells us that before Islam, women used to roam about without *Hijāb* freely, shamelessly and without any controls. Therefore, the earlier Interpreters of the Holy Qur'ān interpreted these Verses in light of the traditions of the former Times of Ignorance. When one reads those interpretations and compares them with the ignorance of the present times, it appears that today people have become even more ignorant than the men in those ancient times.

Mujāhid and Qatādah say that the word *Tabarruj* in this Verse means walking in a lewd way. Muqātil states that *Tabarruj* is when a woman only covers her head with her scarf without covering her neck and chest. Mubarrad says that *Tabarruj* is when a woman reveals her physical attractiveness which she is required to hide. Lais states that *Tabarruj* is when a woman does not hide the beauty of her face and her physical shape and considers it good to reveal it. Abū 'Ubaidah (r.a.) says *Tabarruj* is when a woman exhibits her beauty and her body in a way as to cause sexual excitement in men. 'Allāmah Ibn Jauzī, after quoting the above statements, writes: I believe that coming out of her house and roaming about the streets in itself is sufficient to cause trouble, let alone exhibiting her beauty and her body. (*Ahkāmun-Nisa'*)

All of the above things, explained by the earlier interpreters under the definition of *Tabarruj*, are prevalent today. The daughters of the Muslim society today, with a few exceptions, have even gone far beyond. This is despite the fact that the Prophet (s.a.w.) has said:

شر النساء المتبرجات وهن المنافقات لا يدخل الجنة منهن الا مثل الغراب الأعصم

(سنن بيهقي)

> The worse among the women are those who freely leave their homes without *Hijāb*. They are hypocrites and few of these will enter paradise. (*Sunan Al-Baihaqī*)

It is to dissipate this *Tabarruj* that the Prophet (s.a.w.), while accepting women in Islam, used to make them promise not to engage in *Tabarruj*. (*Tabrānī*).

From the word *Tabarruj* in the above Verse, it is also clear that if it is necessary for a woman to leave her house, she has to hide her beauty. This can be achieved by wearing a *Burqa'* or *Jalbāb*[3] that covers her entire body.

The advocates of women's freedom often object that the Commandments of *Hijāb* in this Verse are only meant for the Wives of the Prophet (s.a.w.), who are the subject of this Verse, and, therefore, do not apply to all women.

In fact, if one reads the complete Verse, it is clear that none of the five Commandments in this Verse are limited only to the Wives of the Prophet (s.a.w.). Even the Commandments in the Verses before and after it are also applicable to all Muslim women. In this Verse, the first Commandment is about the etiquette of speaking with *Ghair-Mahram*, then for women to stay in their homes, then to establish the *Salāt*, then to pay the *Zakāt*, and finally to obey Allah and His Prophet (s.a.w.). Now, who can claim that the Commandments related to *Salāt*, *Zakāt* and obedience of Allah and His Prophet (s.a.w.) in this Verse are also meant only for the Wives of the Prophet (s.a.w.) and that the rest of the women are exempt from these?

The truth is that these Commandments are meant for all Muslim women, although apparently the first subjects of this Verse were the Wives of the Prophet (s.a.w.). This has occurred in the Qur'ān in many places where the initial address is specific

---

[3] *Burqa'* is a cover-all worn on top of their garments by Muslim women in Asia to cover the entire body. *Jalbāb* is the outer sheet or coverlet which a woman wraps around her on top of her garments for the same purpose.

to a person, but the Commandment is applicable to all. Imām Abū Bakr Jassās writes in the interpretation of this Verse:

> This Verse provides a clear argument that women are required to stay in their homes and it is forbidden for them to leave their homes... And all the etiquettes in this Verse were taught to the Wives of the Prophet (s.a.w.) to safeguard their chastity. All Muslim women are required to follow these Commandments. (*Jassās*, vol. 5, p. 230)

'Allāmah Ibn Kathīr writes:

> These are the etiquettes Allah taught the Wives of the Prophet (s.a.w.) and since all the women of Muslim *Ummah* are required to follow their example, these Commandments are applicable to all Muslim women. (*Ibn Kathīr*, vol. 3, p. 483)

Besides, Allah confirmed the purity and chastity of the Wives of the Prophet (s.a.w.) in an entire Ruku' of the Qur'ān, clearly stating:

إِنَّمَا يُرِيدُ اللهُ لِيُذْهِبَ عَنكُمُ الرِّجْسَ أَهْلَ الْبَيْتِ وَ يُطَهِّرَكُمْ تَطْهِيْرًا ۝ (الأحزاب:٣٣)

> Allah only wishes to remove all abomination from you, you Members of the Family, and to make you pure and spotless. (*Sūrah Ahzāb*, v. 33)

When Allah Himself confirmed their purity and chastity, can anyone expect them to engage in sweet talk with men while explaining to them matters of religion? When such a thing is not even thinkable, why then did Allah give them these specific Commandments? The answer is that Allah wanted them to be aware of the natural attraction in a woman's voice and to make a conscious effort to change it with harshness while talking to men so that even this natural delicacy will not become apparent to *Ghair-Mahram*.

The following things are noteworthy here:

1. The Wives of the Prophet (s.a.w.) possess a high status among women. They were cleansed and purified by Allah. No one could even think of them indulging in any sinful activities.

2. وَ أَزْوَاجُهُ أُمَّهَاتُهُمْ "They are the Mothers of the *Ummah* as Allah," Allah proclaimed in *Sūrah Ahzāb*, Verse 6.

3. This proclamation was not merely out of respect for them, but as with real mothers, it was forbidden to marry any of them after the demise of the Prophet (s.a.w.). Allah said:

وَلَآ أَنْ تَنْكِحُوْا أَزْوَاجَهُ مِنْ بَعْدِهِ أَبَدًا إِنَّ ذَالِكُمْ كَانَ عِنْدَاللهِ عَظِيْمًا ۝ (الأحزاب:٥٣)

> ....Nor that you should ever marry his widows after him at any time. Indeed that would be an enormity in the sight of Allah. (*Sūrah Ahzāb*, v. 53)

4. People who spoke to the Wives of the Prophet (s.a.w.) were none other than the Companions whose piety Allah Himself confirmed in the Qur'ān saying: رَضِيَ اللهُ عَنْهُمْ وَ رَضُوْا عَنْهُمْ "These are the ones who are happy with Me and I am happy with them (*Sūrah Bayyinah*, v. 8)." Also: وَكُلًّا وَعَدَاللهُ الْحُسْنٰى "...And all of them we forgave..." (*Sūrah Hadīd*, v. 10)

5. The conversations between the Wives of the Prophet (s.a.w.) and the Companions were nothing more than teaching and learning the matters of religion.

Despite the above facts, Allah commanded the Consorts of the Prophet (s.a.w.) to observe *Hijāb*, and commanded the Companions to talk to them from behind a screen. Then, it is not difficult to see how important it would be for men and women to follow these Commandments in this day and age.

BURQA' OR *JALBĀB*

In the last Verse, Muslim women were asked not to leave their homes without necessity. If they must, they should not go out boldly without *Hijāb* like the women of the olden Days of Ignorance. Further, in *Sūrah Ahzāb*, Allah commanded them to use *Jalbāb* when they came out of their homes:

3. يَٰٓأَيُّهَا ٱلنَّبِيُّ قُل لِّأَزْوَٰجِكَ وَبَنَاتِكَ وَنِسَآءِ ٱلْمُؤْمِنِينَ يُدْنِينَ
عَلَيْهِنَّ مِن جَلَٰبِيبِهِنَّ ذَٰلِكَ أَدْنَىٰٓ أَن يُعْرَفْنَ فَلَا يُؤْذَيْنَ وَكَانَ
ٱللَّهُ غَفُورًا رَّحِيمًا (الاحزاب:٥٩)

> O' Prophet! Tell your Wives and daughters, and the believing women that they should cast (*Yudnīna 'Alaihinna*) their outer garments (*Jalābīb*) over them; so that it is likelier that they will be known and not harmed; and Allah is All-Forgiving, Most Merciful. (*Sūrah Ahzāb*, v. 59)

This Verse is a very important one among the Verses revealed about *Hijāb*, because it clearly states that hiding one's face is included in the Commandment of *Hijāb*. Therefore, the scholars and Interpreters of the Holy Qur'ān have discussed this issue at great length.

Secondly, since this Verse is not specifically addressed only to the Consorts of the Prophet (s.a.w.), there is no room to make excuses regarding its applicability to all women.

Let us look at the literal meaning of the words *JALBĀB* and *YUDNĪNA 'ALAIHINNA* in this Verse.

WHAT IS *JALBĀB*?

JALĀBĪB is the plural form of the word *JALBĀB*. Many different interpretations have been made in explaining *Jalbāb.* In his research of this word, 'Allāmah Ibn Al-Manzūr concludes:

> *Jalbāb* is actually the outer sheet or coverlet which a woman wraps around on top of her garments to cover herself from head to toe. It hides her body completely. (*Lisān-ul Arab*, vol. 1, p. 273)

The root word is *JALBĀB* which is basically used for such things which completely cover something. For example, the blankets we use in cold weather or the darkness of the night which covers all things completely.

The word *Jalbāb* is therefore used for that outer sheet which a woman wraps around on top of her clothes to hide herself from the eyes of strangers.

In interpreting the word, 'Allāmah Ibn Al-Hazam writes:

> In Arabic language, the language of the Prophet (s.a.w.), *Jalbāb* is that outer sheet which covers

> the entire body. A piece of cloth which is too small to cover the entire body could not be called *Jalbāb*. (*Al-Muhalla*, vol. 3, p. 217)

In describing it, Ibn Mas'ūd (r.a.) said that *Jalbāb* is that sheet of cloth which is worn on top of the scarf. Ibn 'Abbās (r.a.) described it as follows:

> Allah commanded Muslim women to pull this sheet on top of them to cover their bodies except one eye, when it is necessary for them to come out of their home. (*Ibn Kathīr*)

Imām Mohammed Bin Sirīn said, "When I asked 'Ubaidah Salmani (r.a.) the meaning of this Verse and how the *Jalbāb* was to be used, he demonstrated it to me by pulling a sheet of cloth over his head to cover his body, leaving his left eye uncovered. This was also the explanation of the word *'ALAIHINNA* in this Verse."

This Verse clearly requires hiding of the face which supports the Commandments in the Verse of *Hijāb*.

The second phrase in this Verse which requires interpretation is *YUDNĪNA 'ALAIHINNA*. 'Allāmah Ālūsī writes:

> (The root word) *ADNA* literally means to bring something closer. Here it means to hang something close to you, or over you, since it is followed by *'ALA* in the phrase. In my opinion, *ADNA* followed by *'ALA* points towards covering themselves with the sheet hanging on top of them in a way so that they can see the road as they walk (*Rūh-ul-Ma'ānī*, vol. 22, pp. 88-89)

After quoting and discussing many interpretations, 'Allāmah Ālūsī concludes:

> All the above discussions deal with explaining the gist (of the term). The apparent meaning of the word *'ALAIHINNA* is clearly to cover one's body completely, although some have interpreted it to mean covering the head and the face, because in the olden Days of Ignorance, women usually left their faces uncovered.

HOW TO WRAP THE SHEET AROUND

Not only did the scholars of the Holy Qur'ān clarify for us that, according to this Verse, it is mandatory for women to wear *Hijāb* and hide their faces, but they also explained exactly how the *Jalbāb* should be worn. The greatest interpreter of the Holy Qur'ān, Ibn 'Abbās (r.a.), has been reported to have mentioned two ways of wearing *Jalbāb*. The first one, where the sheet of cloth should be pulled over on top to cover the body with the exception of one eye, has been already mentioned above. The second method, which allows for keeping both eyes uncovered, has been reported by 'Allāmah Ālūsī as follows:

> Ibn Jarīr and Ibn Al-Munzir described the method of wearing the *Jalbāb* according to Ibn 'Abbās and Qatādah. The sheet should be wrapped from the top covering the forehead, then bringing one side of the sheet to cover the face below the eyes so that most of the face and the upper body is covered. This will leave both the eyes uncovered (which is acceptable under necessity). (*Rūh-ul-Ma'ānī*, vol. 22, p. 89)

Many other scholars, such as Mohammed Bin Sīrīn, 'Allāmah Ibn Jarīr, Imām Suddī, Imām Abūbakr Jassās, Imām Wāhidī, and

'Allāmah Ibn Sa'd Mohammed Bin Ka'b Kurazī, have described the use of *Jalbāb* in more or less the same way as the two ways described by Ibn 'Abbās (r.a.).

In addition to the scholars mentioned above, all interpreters of the Holy Qur'ān, from the time of the Prophet (s.a.w.) to the present day, have consistently adhered to the same interpretation of this Verse, i.e., women are required to cover themselves when coming out of their homes and that hiding of the face is included in the *Hijāb*. To quote all these scholars would make this document unnecessarily long, but following are some examples:

> 'Allāmah Ibn Jarīr writes:
>
> In this Verse, Allah is commanding the Prophet (s.a.w.) to ask his Wives, his daughters and to all Muslim women that they should not dress like slave girls leaving their heads and faces uncovered when they come out of their homes. Instead, they should cover themselves with a cloak covering their faces so that nobody will stand in their way and everyone will know that they are respectable folks. (*Tafsīr Ibn Jarīr*, vol. 22, p. 29)
>
> 'Allāmah Nīshāpūrī writes:
>
> In the early days of Islam, all women used to come out dressed in knee-length shirts and scarves as was the tradition in the former Days of Ignorance. There was no difference in the dresses of street women and those from respectable families. Then Allah commanded (Muslim women) to cover their heads and faces so that people would differentiate them from the street women. (*Ahkām-ul Qur'ān*, vol. 4, p. 354)

'Allāmah Abū Hayyān states:

> The advantage in observing *Hijāb* is that these women are recognized as pious and respectable. Thus, the perverts would not be after them and the women would not have to face unpleasantness. Nobody will dare follow and make advances to a woman who has completely concealed herself as opposed to the one who has come out nicely decorated without *Hijāb*; the malicious and evil-minded folks will associate great hopes with such women. (*Al-Bahr-ul Muhīt*, vol. 7, p. 250)

These quotations are taken from some of the well-known Interpreters of the Holy Qur'ān. Otherwise, almost all the scholars of the Holy Qur'ān have been interpreting this Verse to include hiding of the face in the Commandment of *Hijāb*. It is also noteworthy that among these scholars are the followers of all the four schools of thought. Thus, regardless of whether they are Hanafī, Shāf'ī, Humbalī or Mālikī, all include hiding of the face in the Commandment of *Hijāb* without any disagreement.

And, this is not a theoretical matter. We find from the Ahādīth and other narrations that all women, including the Wives of the Prophet (s.a.w.), immediately implemented this Commandment after the Revelation of this Verse, and the use of *Jalbāb* and *Hijāb* by women quickly became the norm of the Muslim society. Actually, it was exemplary how readily the Muslim women obeyed and practiced it. Imām Abdul Razzāq narrated from Ummi Salamah (r.a.):

> عن أم سلمه قالت لمانزل يدنين عليهن من جلا بيبهن خرج نساءالأنصار كان علي رؤوسهن الغربان من السكينه و عليهن اكسيه سوع يلبسنها
> (روح المعاني، ج ٢٢، ص ٨٩)

After the Revelation of this Verse, the ladies of Ansar used to come out of their homes and walk with such dignity as if there were birds sitting on their heads (which would fly away if they walked any faster). And, they used to cover themselves with big black cloaks.

It should be noted here that the modern day *Burqa'* (which is used in some countries by Muslim women) also serves as *Jalbāb*. It is this *Hijāb*, customary among Muslim women since the beginning of Islam, which is now being abolished by those who have been influenced by the western thinking. To accomplish this, they interpret the Holy Qur'ān and Ahādīth according to their own desires thereby going astray themselves and leading others on the same path. May Allah guide us and protect us from these mischiefs.

THE COMMANDMENT FOR PROTECTING GAZE AND HIDING ADORNMENT

Not only did Islam command women to stay home, to not talk to *Ghair-Mahram* men seductively, and to cover themselves with cloaks, it barricaded all those roads from where carnal excitement and bad thoughts may attack human beings. Thus, Allah said (in the Holy Qur'ān):

4. قُل لِّلْمُؤْمِنِينَ يَغُضُّوا مِنْ أَبْصَارِهِمْ وَيَحْفَظُوا فُرُوجَهُمْ ذَٰلِكَ
أَزْكَىٰ لَهُمْ إِنَّ اللَّهَ خَبِيرٌ بِمَا يَصْنَعُونَ ۝ وَقُل لِّلْمُؤْمِنَاتِ يَغْضُضْنَ
مِنْ أَبْصَارِهِنَّ وَيَحْفَظْنَ فُرُوجَهُنَّ وَلَا يُبْدِينَ زِينَتَهُنَّ إِلَّا مَا
ظَهَرَ مِنْهَا وَلْيَضْرِبْنَ بِخُمُرِهِنَّ عَلَىٰ جُيُوبِهِنَّ وَلَا يُبْدِينَ
زِينَتَهُنَّ إِلَّا لِبُعُولَتِهِنَّ أَوْ آبَائِهِنَّ أَوْ آبَاءِ بُعُولَتِهِنَّ أَوْ أَبْنَائِهِنَّ
أَوْ أَبْنَاءِ بُعُولَتِهِنَّ أَوْ إِخْوَانِهِنَّ أَوْ بَنِي إِخْوَانِهِنَّ أَوْ بَنِي أَخَوَاتِهِنَّ
أَوْ نِسَائِهِنَّ أَوْ مَا مَلَكَتْ أَيْمَانُهُنَّ أَوِ التَّابِعِينَ غَيْرِ أُولِي الْإِرْبَةِ
مِنَ الرِّجَالِ أَوِ الطِّفْلِ الَّذِينَ لَمْ يَظْهَرُوا عَلَىٰ عَوْرَاتِ النِّسَاءِ

وَلَا يَضْرِبْنَ بِأَرْجُلِهِنَّ لِيُعْلَمَ مَا يُخْفِينَ مِن زِينَتِهِنَّ وَتُوبُوا
إِلَى اللَّهِ جَمِيعًا أَيُّهَ الْمُؤْمِنُونَ لَعَلَّكُمْ تُفْلِحُونَ ۝ وَأَنكِحُوا الْأَيَامَىٰ

(النور: ٣١-٣٠)

Say to the believing men that they should lower their gaze and guard their modesty; that will make for greater purity for them; and Allah is well acquainted with all that they do. And say to the believing women that they should lower their gaze and guard their modesty; that they should not display their beauty and ornaments except what (must ordinarily) appear thereof; that they should draw their veils over their bosoms and not display their beauty except to their husbands, their fathers, their fathers-in-law, their sons, their step sons, their brothers or their brothers' sons, or their sisters' sons, or their women, or the slaves whom their right hands possess, or male servants free of physical needs, or small children who have no sense of the shame of sex; and that they should not strike their feet in order to draw attention to their hidden ornaments. And O you Believers! Turn you all together towards Allah, that you may attain Bliss. (*Sūrah Nūr*, v. 30-31)

Before going into the details of the Commandments contained in the above two Verses, it will be useful to know that the very first Verse containing the Commandments of *Hijāb* was the one which was mentioned in the beginning of this chapter, i.e., the Verse 53 of *Sūrah Ahzāb* which was revealed at the time of the wedding of Zainab Bint Jahash (r.a.) to the Prophet (s.a.w.). Scholars have estimated that this Verse was revealed in either the 3rd or 5th year of Hijrah. Imām Ibn Kathīr and 'Allāmah Shaukānī believed it to be in the 5th year of Hijra. However, there has been a consensus among all scholars about this Verse being the very first one related to the Commandments of *Hijāb*.

The above two Verses of *Sūrah Nūr* were revealed at the time of the incident of *Ifk* which occurred upon the return of the Prophet (s.a.w.) from the battle of Banī Al-Mustaliq. This battle took place in the 6th year of Hijra, which tells us that these two Verses were revealed after the Verses of *Sūrah Ahzāb*. Thus, the Commandments of *Hijāb* were implemented when the Verses in *Sūrah Ahzāb* were revealed (which was a year before the above two Verses).

These Verses further contain the following Commandments:

1. LOWERING THE EYES (GHADD AL-BASAR): The word *Yaghuddu* in the above Verses comes from the root word *Ghadd* which means to lower, to regulate, to suppress (*Mufaradāt-ul Qur'ān*). To lower the eyes in this context means to turn away the eyes from everything forbidden (*Tafsīr Ibn Kathīr*). Included in this is looking at a woman with bad intentions and also looking at a woman with no specific intention. As well, it includes looking at those parts of the body of a man or woman which are defined as private (*Satr*). However, necessities such as medical treatment, are exempt from it. Similarly, to peek into people's houses and to use the eyes in seeing all such things that the religion has forbidden are included under this Commandment.

2. GUARDING THE MODESTY (PRIVATE PARTS): This implies restraining oneself from all forbidden means to satisfy one's sexual desires. Included in this are adultery, rape, masturbation, homosexuality, lesbianism, etc.

With a little analysis, it becomes clear that the intent in these Verses is to stop people from all forbidden means of satisfying sexual desires. The beginning and the end points were clearly pointed out (i.e., looking at others with bad intentions and guarding the private parts), and everything in between automatically became part of this Commandment. The sexual excitement and mischief indeed begins from freely looking at the opposite sex, and its potential end is indulging in adultery and rape. In between these extremes are sexual fantasies, lewd talk, touching, fondling, etc. 'Allāmah Ibn Kathīr quotes 'Ubaidah (r.a.):

كل ماعصي الله به كبيرة و قد ذكرالطرفن
(تفسيرابن كثير)

> Everything which is in disobedience of Allah is a major sin. In this Verse, the beginning and the end point of this sin have been identified. (*Tafsīr Ibn Kathīr*)

3. CONCEALING THE BEAUTY AND ORNAMENTS: What does the word *Zīnat* mean? Maulānā Muhammad Idrīs Kāndhalvī writes in the interpretation of this Verse:

> *Zīnat* means beautification, whether it is natural such as face, hands and body, or artificial and intentional such as, clothes, jewelry and make-up. All of these form the apparent beauty of a woman and are included in the meaning of إِلَّا مَا ظَهَرَ مِنْهَا. All of these things, therefore, should be concealed from everyone except the *Mahārim* (those who have been exempted). These have been described in the next Verse. The Commandments in this Verse are mainly related

> to women's *Satr*, i.e., an explanation of what parts of a woman's body and her beauty must be concealed from others. In the next Verse, exceptions have been listed about the people in front of whom she does not have to observe these restrictions. These are twelve. (*Ma'ārif-ul Qur'ān*)

Muftī Muhammad Shafī's interpretation of this Verse reads:

> In the beginning of this Verse, women were asked not to reveal their beauty. In this part of the Verse, they have been asked to conceal their natural beauty as well by covering it with their scarves. The purpose here was also to eradicate the tradition, which was prevalent in the Days of Ignorance, whereby women use to put their scarves on their heads with the sides hanging on the back. This left their ears, neck, collar, and chest exposed. Therefore, Muslim women were asked here not to wear their scarves in this manner, but to wrap the two sides of it closely on top of their chests covering all these parts of the body.

Next, those men are described with whom *Hijāb* is not required. There are two reasons for these exceptions.

First, there is no danger of any mischief from these men, as they are the *Mahārim*[4]. By nature, these men are the

---

[4] *Mahārim* is plural of the word *Mahram*. A *Mahram* is a man with whom marriage is forbidden and, therefore, women are not required to observe *Hijāb* in front of them. Examples of such men are father, brother, and uncle.

protectors of their women's honour. Second, they live with these women in the same house which also dictates that they be exempted from these restrictions. It is also important to remember that with the exception of the husband, *Satr* must be observed with the rest of these *Mahārim* men. Exposing of *Satr*, which is not permissible even in *Salāt*, is forbidden with the *Mahārim* as well.

Eight *Mahārim* and four other kinds of men have been exempted in this Verse from the Commandment of *Hijāb*. Seven of these *Mahārim* were mentioned before in the Verse of *Hijāb* in *Sūrah Ahzāb*. Five other exceptions were mentioned in this Verse.

It should also be kept in mind that the word *Mahram* has been used here in its common meaning and includes the husband. The interpretation of *Mahram* by the scholars, which means "a man with whom marriage is forbidden," is not meant here.

1. Husband: A wife is not required to observe *Hijāb* of any part of her body with her husband. However, to look at the private parts unnecessarily is not preferable. 'Āishah (r.a.) stated that the Prophet (s.a.w.) never looked at her private parts nor did she look at his.

2. Father: The grandfather and the great grandfather are also included in this category.

3. Father-in-Law: The grand father-in-law and the great grandfather-in-law are included here as well.

4. Sons: The real sons.

5. Step-sons.

6. Real and step-brothers. However, cousin brothers, all of whom are considered *Ghair-Mahram*, are not included in this category.

7. Sons of the real or step brothers.

8. Sons of real and step sisters. Cousin sisters are not included in here.

The above are the eight kinds of *Mahārim*.

9. Women: *Hijāb* does not need to be observed with other Muslim women either, but *Satr* cannot be exposed to them as well. However, for the purpose of medical treatment, it is permissible.

10. Their women attendants or servants: According to the majority of scholars, male servants are not included in this category. *Hijāb* must be observed with male servants in the same way as with other *Ghair-Mahram* men.

11. Men who have no interest or desire for women: These are the men who, because of their mental or physical condition, have no interest or desire left in them for the opposite sex.

12. Immature children: Those who have not reached puberty and have not developed an interest or knowledge of the specific matters related to sex and women. Those children who have such knowledge and interest, regardless of their age, will not be included in this category.

4. CONCEALING THE SOUND: The fourth important issue that has been discussed in this Verse pertains to the sound. Women have been asked not to walk with a heavy foot so as to draw attention of men through the sounds of their jewelry.

According to this, to attach any such things to the jewelry which make noise, or to wear jewelry on top of each other producing noise, or to walk in a way so as to create noise of the jewelry which may be heard by *Ghair-Mahram* men, are all forbidden.

From this Verse, many jurists have inferred that if it is forbidden to have the *Ghair-Mahram* men hear the sounds made by pieces of jewelry, it is certainly forbidden for *Ghair-Mahram* men to hear the voice of women. That is why, these jurists have included the voice of a woman in the definition of *Satr*.

Now whether the voice of a woman in itself is a part of her *Satr* is a controversial issue. Imām Shāf'ī has not included it in the definition of *Satr* for women. There is a difference of opinion among the followers of Imām Abū Hanīfah. Ibn Hammām has included it in *Satr* which is why it is not preferable for a woman to call Adhān. However, it is evident from Ahādīth that the Wives of the Prophet (s.a.w.) spoke with the *Ghair-Mahram* men from behind a curtain even after the Revelation of the Verse of *Hijāb*. From all of this, it seems that where it has the potential to create *Fitnah* (mischief) for both the men and women, it is forbidden. Where there is no such likelihood, it is permissible for a woman to speak with a *Ghair-Mahram* man. To be on the safe side though, it is preferable that women don't talk to *Ghair-Mahram* men unnecessarily.

Imām Jassās, in the interpretation of this Verse, wrote:

> When Allah has included the sounds of jewelry worn by a woman in the expression of her beauty, it would also be forbidden for a woman to wear colourful and decorated outer garments

(like a *Jalbāb* or *Burqa'*, when she is among the *Ghair-Mahram* men).

تُوبُوْا اِلَى اللهِ جَمِيْعًا أَيُّهَ الْمُؤْمِنُوْن "And O you Believers, turn you all together towards Allah, so that you may attain Bliss." After commanding men to lower their gaze and women to observe *Hijāb* with *Ghair-Mahram* men, Allah instructed all men and women to turn to Him for forgiveness for their shortcomings, and to make a firm determination not to disobey Allah again. (*Ma'ārif-ul Qur'ān*, vol. 6, p. 394)

A DANGEROUS MISUNDERSTANDING

In fact, all the above Commands in these Verses of *Sūrah Nūr* are intended to prevent adultery and rape. Thus, these Commands provide the best preventative strategies and treatment for the protection of men's and women's honour. Also, these Commands are unsurpassable for shaping character and cleansing the inner self (*Tazkiyah-i-Bātin*).

However, those whose eyes are blinded with the veil of sexual excitement and hunger are not able to see the beauty of these Verses. These lovers of western values and prisoners of their own carnal desires, who wish to do away with these Commands of maintaining the honour, try to present the meaning of the phrase, "Except what is apparent outwardly (or what must appear ordinarily)," in this Verse in a way that suits their purpose. They claim that since some of the Companions and their followers have been reported to interpret this phrase as meaning the face and hands, that it is all right for women to roam around publicly with their faces uncovered. This is a misunderstanding which is being promoted for the sheer purpose of following the western values and obtaining freedom from the dictates of the religion.

As it has been explained before, the phrase, "Except what is apparent outwardly," is meant to clarify that a woman is allowed to expose her face and hands because some needs and circumstances necessitate it. It does not talk about those needs and circumstances. The next part of this Verse, beginning with, "They should draw their veils over their bosoms and not display their beauty except....," describes the limits and boundaries of when and in front of whom can a woman expose her face and hands. It clearly states that women are not to expose their face and hands except in front of *Mahārim* men.

Besides, if a woman's face and hands were exempt from the Command of concealing her beauty and ornaments, then why was it necessary to list, in the next part of the Verse, those people in front of whom she could expose her face and hands? The fact is that the Verse, "They should not display their beauty and ornaments except what (must ordinarily) appear thereof," deals with the unexposable parts of a woman's body (*Satr*) and not with *Hijāb*. The next part of the Verse talks about *Hijāb* and the people in front of whom she can come freely with her face and hands exposed, i.e., without *Hijāb*. Thus, Interpreters of the Holy Qur'ān, such as, Ibn 'Abbās, Ibn Jarīr and Ibn Kathīr have interpreted the Verse accordingly. Ibn Kathīr, for example, writes:

> In this Verse, Allah listed the *Mahārim* of a woman and said that although she could expose her beauty in front of these *Mahārim*, but in doing so the intent must not be to show off her adornment. (*Tafsīr Ibn Kathīr*, vol. 3, p. 284)

Secondly, if women were allowed to go freely with their faces exposed in front of everyone, why was it necessary to command them to guard their eyes (*Ghadd Al-Basar*) - وَقُلْ لِلْمُؤْمِنَاتِ يَغْضُضْنَ مِنْ أَبْصَارِهِنَّ, "And say to the believing women that they should lower their gaze"?

Third, if it was permissible for women to go freely in front of anyone with their faces exposed, why did Allah commanded in *Sūrah Nūr* to seek permission before entering a household - يٰاَيُّهَاالَّذِيْنَ آمَنُوْا لَا تَدْخُلُوْا بُيُوْتًا غَيْرَ بُيُوْتِكُمْ حَتّٰي تَسْتَأْنِسُوْا... "O you who believe! Enter not houses other than your own, until you have asked permission....." (*Sūrah Nūr*, v. 27)

Fourth, Allah commanded women: وَ قَرْنَ فِيْ بُيُوْتِكُنَّ وَلَا تَبَرَّجْنَ تَبَرُّجَ الْجَاهِلِيَّةِالْأُوْلٰي "And stay quietly in your houses, and make not a dazzling display, like that of the former Times of Ignorance." If women could go around freely with their faces exposed, why was this Command necessary?

Fifth, Allah also commanded: وَ إِذَا سَأَلْتُمُوْهُنَّ مَتَاعًافَسْئَلُوْهُنَّ مِنْ وَرَآءِ حِجَابٍ ذَالِكُمْ أَطْهَرُ لِقُلُوْبِكُمْ وَ قُلُوْبِهِنَّ "And when you ask (his Wives) for anything you need, ask them from behind a screen; that makes for greater purity for your hearts and for theirs." (*Sūrah Ahzāb*, v. 53) So, we find out that asking them from behind a screen maintains the purity of hearts and talking to them without any screen may cause contamination of hearts.

Sixth, even if a woman needs to talk to a man from behind a screen, she has been commanded to: فَلَا تَخْضَعْنَ بِالْقَوْلِ فَيَطْمَعَ الَّذِيْ فِيْ قَلْبِهٖ مَرَضٌ وَ قُلْنَ قَوْلاً مَعْرُوْفاً "Be not too complaisant of speech, lest one in whose heart is a disease should be moved with desire." (Ibid. v. 32) If it was permissible for a woman to go freely in front of men, what was the need for this Command?

Seventh, Allah also commanded women: وَلَا يَضْرِبْنَ بِأَرْجُلِهِنَّ لِيُعْلَمَ مَا يُخْفِيْنَ مِنْ زِيْنَتِهِنَّ "And that they should not strike their feet in order to draw attention to their hidden ornaments" (*Sūrah Nūr*, v. 31), because if their attention was drawn to them, it may excite their desires creating the possibility of *Fitnah.*

Now, in the light of all of the above, who, in their right mind, would claim that Islamic *Sharī'ah* which has attempted to close all possible ways to lewdness and sexual excitement and freedom, will permit women to go freely in front of all with their faces exposed, thereby reopening all those paths again?

SEEKING PERMISSION BEFORE ENTERING A HOUSE

With respect to *Hijāb*, Islamic *Sharī'ah* also commanded not to enter each other's houses without seeking permission in order to preserve the privacy and sanctity of the household. Allah says:

5. يَٰٓأَيُّهَا ٱلَّذِينَ ءَامَنُوا۟ لَا تَدْخُلُوا۟ بُيُوتًا غَيْرَ بُيُوتِكُمْ حَتَّىٰ تَسْتَأْنِسُوا۟
وَتُسَلِّمُوا۟ عَلَىٰٓ أَهْلِهَا ذَٰلِكُمْ خَيْرٌ لَّكُمْ لَعَلَّكُمْ تَذَكَّرُونَ

(النور:٢٧)

> O you who believe! do not enter houses other than your own until you have asked permission and saluted the dwellers therein; that is best for you, (Allah admonishes you) so that you may heed. (*Sūrah Nūr*, v. 27)

One of the major reasons for the above Commandment is also to ensure that the ladies of the house may move to the inner quarters of the house before a *Ghair-Mahram* stranger walks in.

FOR ELDERLY WOMEN

For elderly women, who no longer have sexual desires or the attraction, there is, however, some concession made in these requirements. Allah says:

6.

يٰأَيُّهَا الَّذِيْنَ اٰمَنُوْا لِيَسْتَأْذِنْكُمُ الَّذِيْنَ مَلَكَتْ أَيْمَانُكُمْ
وَالَّذِيْنَ لَمْ يَبْلُغُوا الْحُلُمَ مِنْكُمْ ثَلٰثَ مَرّٰتٍ مِنْ قَبْلِ
صَلٰوةِ الْفَجْرِ وَ حِيْنَ تَضَعُوْنَ ثِيَابَكُمْ مِنَ الظَّهِيْرَةِ وَ مِنْ
بَعْدِ صَلٰوةِ الْعِشَآءِ ثَلٰثُ عَوْرَاتٍ لَكُمْ لَيْسَ عَلَيْكُمْ وَلَا عَلَيْهِمْ
جُنَاحٌ بَعْدَهُنَّ طَوّٰفُوْنَ عَلَيْكُمْ بَعْضُكُمْ عَلٰي بَعْضٍ كَذٰلِكَ
يُبَيِّنُ اللهُ لَكُمُ الْاٰيٰتِ وَاللهُ عَلِيْمٌ حَكِيْمٌ ○ وَ إِذَا بَلَغَ
الْأَطْفَالُ مِنْكُمُ الْحُلُمَ فَلْيَسْتَأْذِنُوْا كَمَا اسْتَأْذَنَ الَّذِيْنَ مِنْ
قَبْلِهِمْ كَذٰلِكَ يُبَيِّنُ اللهُ لَكُمْ اٰيٰتِهٖ وَاللهُ عَلِيْمٌ حَكِيْمٌ ○
وَالْقَوَاعِدُ مِنَ النِّسَآءِ الّٰتِيْ لَا يَرْجُوْنَ نِكَاحًا فَلَيْسَ عَلَيْهِنَّ
جُنَاحٌ أَنْ يَّضَعْنَ ثِيَابَهُنَّ غَيْرَ مُتَبَرِّجٰتٍ بِزِيْنَةٍ وَ أَنْ
يَّسْتَعْفِفْنَ خَيْرٌ لَّهُنَّ وَاللهُ سَمِيْعٌ عَلِيْمٌ ○

(النور: ٦٠-٥٨)

O you who believe! Let those whom your right hands possess and the (children) among you who have not come of age ask your permission (before they come to your presence) on three occasions: before the *Fajr* prayer, the time when you remove your clothes for the noonday heat, and after the Isha prayer; these are your three times of undress; outside those times it is not wrong for you, or for them, to move about attending to each other; thus does Allah make clear the Signs to you; for Allah is Full of Knowledge and Wisdom.

But when the children among you come of age let them (also) ask for permission as do those senior to them (in age); thus does Allah make

> clear His Signs to you; for Allah is Full of Knowledge and Wisdom.
>
> Such elderly women as are past the prospect of marriage, there is no blame on them if they lay aside their (outer) garments provided they make not a wilful display of their beauty, but it is best for them to be modest, and Allah is the One Who sees and knows all things. (*Sūrah Nūr*, v. 58-60)

The first two Verses above allow small children and slaves to move about freely in the house with the exception of the specified times. Thus, women are also free to be around them without their outer robes.

The third Verse provides concession for such elderly women who no longer have any desire for marriage or attraction for men, and who can, therefore, take off their outer garments (*Burqa'*, *Hijāb*, robes, etc.) in front of men other than *Mahārim* provided that they do not display their make-up. Although the concession was granted, it was reminded that the preferable thing to do is to be modest.

SUMMARY

In conclusion, all the Verses mentioned above from the Holy Qur'ān may be summarized as follows:

1. Women should not leave their homes unless it is absolutely necessary.

2. If they must leave their home, they should wrap themselves in outer cloaks (*Burqa' or Jalbāb*) so as not to expose any part of their bodies.

3. Men and women should not look at each other without utmost necessity.

4. If men need to talk to women, they should do so from behind a screen (curtain).

5. When women need to talk to men, they should do so from behind a screen and not speak in a pleasant and overly friendly manner.

6. Women may keep their face, hands, and feet uncovered in front of *Mahārim* normally, but they should not display the rest of their body parts and should maintain the requirements of *Satr* all the time.

CHAPTER TWO

EVIDENCE FROM AHĀDĪTH

Many Ahādīth have already been mentioned in chapter one under the evidence from the Holy Qur'ān. The purpose here is not to repeat those Ahādīth, but to mention only a few more. To cover all the Ahādīth in this regard is neither possible for an incapable person like me nor is it necessary, for I believe that even the evidence from the Holy Qur'ān alone is sufficient for one who wishes to follow it; and for those who do not wish to abide by the Divine Law, even the largest collections of the Qur'ānic Verses and Ahādīth will not suffice. In these modern times, we witness that men and women gather together freely in the name of studying the Holy Qur'ān and read these Commandments, but are completely unaffected by them. It is as if they make a mockery of Allah's Commandments by sitting together without any *Hijāb* or partition. For such people, the Prophet (s.a.w.) has been reported to have said, "Many who read the Holy Qur'ān are such people that the Holy Qur'ān itself curses them."

First of all, I will mention some Ahādīth which show us how the female Companions of the Prophet (s.a.w.) vigilantly observed *Hijāb*. There was no difference among them in this regard. They observed *Hijāb* with all men including the Prophet (s.a.w.). They covered their entire bodies including their faces.

THE *HIJĀB* OF THE FEMALE COMPANIONS OF THE PROPHET

In a long Hadīth, 'Āishah (r.a.) reports that:

1.

عن عائشه رضي الله عنها قالت اومت امراة من وراء ستر بيدها كتاب الي رسول الله صلي الله عليه وسلم فقبض النبي صلي الله عليه وسلم يده فقال ما ادري ايد رجل ام يد امرة قالت بل يد امراة قال لو كنت امراة لغيرت اظفارك بالحناء (ابوداؤد، نسائ)

A woman extended her hand from behind a curtain to hand a piece of paper to the Prophet (s.a.w.). The Prophet (s.a.w.) pulled his hand back and said, "I don't know if it is a man's or a woman's hand." She said that it was a woman's hand. The Prophet (s.a.w.) responded, "If you were a woman, you would have coloured your nails with henna." (*Abū Dāwūd, Nasāī*)

This Hadīth is a clear evidence that the female Companions of the Prophet (s.a.w.) used to observe *Hijāb* in front of him, which is why the woman extended her hand from behind the curtain. If it was acceptable for women to come without *Hijāb* in front of men, there was no need for it. Besides, if such *Hijāb* was against the *Sharī'ah* of Islam, the Prophet (s.a.w.) would have certainly pointed it out to her so that it would not have led others astray.

OBSERVANCE OF *HIJĀB* EVEN IN DISTRESS

2.

عن قيس بن شماس رضي الله عنه قال جاءت امرأة الي النبي صلي الله عليه وسلم يقال لها ام خلاد وهي منتقبه فسالت عن ابنها و هو مقتول فقال لها بعض اصحاب النبي صلي الله عليه وسلم جئت تسالين عن ابنك و انت منتقبه فقالت إن ارزأ ابني فلن ارزأ حيائ فقال رسول الله صلي الله عليه وسلم ابنك له اجر شهيدين قالت ولم ذاك يارسول الله فقال لانه قتله اهل الكتاب (ابوداؤد، ج١ ص٣٢٦)

Qais Bin Shammas (r.a.) reported that a female Companion of the Prophet (s.a.w.), whose name was Ummi Khālid, came to see the Prophet (s.a.w.) to inquire about her son who had been martyred in a battle. She was hiding her face behind a veil. One of the Companions asked her, "You have come to inquire about your martyred son and you have covered your face with a veil?" She responded, "I am distressed by the loss of my son, I don't wish to be distressed by the loss of my shyness (*Hayā*)[5] as well." The Prophet (s.a.w.) said to her, "Your son will have the rewards of two martyrs." She asked him, "How come O Prophet of Allah?" He responded, "Because he was killed by the People of the Book." (*Abū Dāwūd*, vol. 1, p. 326)

From the above Hadīth while it is evident that Ummi Khālid (r.a.) covered her face in front of the Companions and the Prophet (s.a.w.), we also note how high a standard women had reached in following the Commandments of *Hijāb*. This woman, despite the distress of losing her son, showed high loyalty to the Commands of Allah, and equated the possible distress of losing her *Hayā* to losing her son.

We also learn from this Hadīth that the Commands of *Hijāb* are essential regardless of the circumstances of sorrow or happiness. Now a days some people believe that under distressing or jubilant circumstances, a person is exempt from following the Divine Law and he/she is not required to follow the *Sharī'ah*. This is clearly a great ignorance. We see women

---

[5] Literally, *Hayā* means Shyness. As an Islamic term, *Hayā* implies that shyness which a person feels before his own conscience and before Allah.

attending funerals and even joining a funeral procession to the graveyard without *Hijāb*, not observing *Hijāb* in weddings, and travelling without *Hijāb*. All of these are forbidden.

OBSERVING *HIJĀB* WHILE MAKING *BAI'AH*[6]

The Prophet (s.a.w.) himself followed the Commands of *Hijāb* with *Ghair-Mahram* women. Like men, women also used to make *Bai'ah* with him. With men, he used to hold their hands in his while making *Bai'ah*, but with women he made *Bai'ah* from behind a curtain without holding their hands since holding a *Ghair-Mahram* woman's hand is as equally forbidden as looking at her.

3.

عن اميمه بنت رقيقه رضي الله عنهاً قالت اتيت رسول
الله صلي الله غليه وسلم في نسوة بايعنه علي الاسلام
فقلناله يار سول الله (صلي الله عليه وسلم) نبايعك علي
ان لا نشرك بالله شيأ ولا نسرق ولا نزني ولا نقتل
اولادنا ولا ناتي ببهتان نفترينه بين ايدينا وارجلنا ولا
نعصينك في معروف قال رسول الله صلي الله عليه وسلم
فيمااستطعن و اطقتن قالت فقلن الله و رسوله ارحم بنا
من انفسنا هلم نبايعك يارسول الله فقال رسول الله صلي
الله عليه وسلم اني لا اصافح النساء انما قولي لمائة
امرأة كقولي لامرأة واحدة او مثل قولي لامرأة واحدة
(موطا امام مالك)

Umaimah (r.a.) reported: I and some other women came to the Prophet (s.a.w.) to make *Bai'ah* on Islam. The women said, "O Prophet of Allah, we make *Bai'ah* with you on the following conditions - that we will not associate anyone with Allah; that we will not steal; that

---

[6] The term *Bai'ah* means to make an oath of allegiance to submit and obey.

> we will not indulge in fornication and adultery (*Zinā*), that we will not kill our offspring, that we will not wrongfully ascribe our illegitimate children to our husbands; and that we will not disobey you in doing good deeds." The Prophet (s.a.w.) said to them, "And say that you will follow all these to the best of your ability." The women responded, "Allah and His Prophet are more merciful on us than we are on ourselves; make *Bai'ah* with us." The Prophet (s.a.w.) said to them, "I don't shake hands with women; when I said to you (what I just said), it is as if I had said it to one hundred women." (*Mu'attā Imām Mālik*, Chapter - *Bai'ah*)

With respect to making *Bai'ah* with women, 'Āishah (r.a.) provides further clarification.

From among women, whoever agreed to these conditions, the Prophet (s.a.w.) said to her, "I made *Bai'ah* with you." By Allah, his hands never touched a woman's hand even at the time of making *Bai'ah* with them. He used to make *Bai'ah* with women verbally and then he used to say to them: قد بايعتك "I made *Bai'ah* with you." (*Bukhārī*, the Book of *Tafsīr*)

Both of these Ahādīth clearly show that the Prophet (s.a.w.), the mentor of all mankind, never touched a woman's hand even at the time of making *Bai'ah*. When women came to him for this purpose, he made *Bai'ah* with them verbally. When they insisted upon holding his hand, he told them: اني لا اصافح النساء "I do not shake hands with women." When *Bai'ah* may be made verbally with women, why should one hold their hands?

OBSERVING *HIJĀB* IN FRONT OF THE COMPANIONS OF THE PROPHET

It is clear from the above Ahādīth that the female Companions observed *Hijāb* strictly, even in front of the Prophet (s.a.w.). Similarly, the Wives of the Prophet (s.a.w.), although considered as the Mothers of the *Ummah*, observed strict *Hijāb* in front of all the Companions of the Prophet (s.a.w.). Thus, 'Āishah (r.a.) states in the detailed Hadīth about the incident of *Ifk*:

4.

فخرجت معه بعد ما انزل الحجاب.... فلما اخذوا براس البعير فانطلقوا به فرجعت الي المعسكر و ما فيه داع ولا مجيب قد انطلق الناس فتلفعت بجلبابي ثم اضطجعت في مكاني اذ مربي صفوان بن المعطل السلمي و كان قد تخلف عن المعسكر لبعض حاجاته فلم يبت مع الناس فراي سوادي فاقبل حتي وقف علي فعرفني حين رأني و كان قد رأني قبل ان يضرب الحجاب فاستيقظت باستر جاعه حين عرفني فخمرت وجهي بجلبابي (مسلم)

I accompanied the Prophet (s.a.w.) to the battle of *Ifk* after the Revelation of the Verses of *Hijāb*..... I arrived back at the army camp after he left with my camel. There was no one left to call or answer. Everyone had left with the army. I covered myself with my shawl and lied down. A little while later, Safwān Bin Mu'attal passed by me. He was left behind due to some personal reason and had not spent the night with the rest. When he saw me, he came near and recognized me as he had seen me before the Revelation of the Verses of *Hijāb*. He recited loudly: Innā

Lillāhi Wa Innā Ilaihi Rājiūn[7] His voice woke me up and I covered my face immediately with my shawl. (*Muslim*, Book of *Taubah*)

This Hadīth proves in many ways that the Wives of the Prophet (s.a.w.) used to observe *Hijāb*.

First, the reason why 'Āishah (r.a.) was left behind in the jungle when the army left, was clearly the fact that their *Hijāb* was not limited to *Burqa'* or wrapping a shawl around. Instead, they used to travel in a palanquin (*Haudaj*) [8] mounted on a camel's back. In this incident, when the army was ready to march, the servants carried the *Haudaj* and mounted it on the camel thinking that 'Āishah (r.a.) was in it (she had a very slim built in those days), while she had left the *Haudaj* in the dark to answer the call of nature. Thus, the army left and she was left alone in the jungle. The servants could not look inside the *Haudaj* to ensure that she was there because it was no longer permissible to do so after the Revelation of the Verses of *Hijāb*.

This incident also strongly confirms the fact that women generally used to stay in their homes and used the *Haudaj* while travelling, which served as an enclosure for them.

The statement by 'Āishah (r.a.) that Safwān Bin Mo'attal recognized her because he had seen her before the Commandments of *Hijāb*, also points to the fact that it was no longer possible for anyone to see the Wives of the Prophet (s.a.w.) after these Commands were revealed. She also stated that as soon as she woke up by his voice, she covered her face

---

[7] A Verse from Qur'ān meaning, 'We all belong to Allah and to Him shall we return'. This Verse is recited upon facing all distressful events.

[8] A *Haudaj* (palanquin) was like a little covered room which was mounted on the back of a camel. Women used to travel in it.

with her shawl which clearly proves that it was necessary to cover her face as part of *Hijāb*.

The fact that the Wives of the Prophet (s.a.w.), in spite of being considered the Mothers of the *Ummah*, used to observe *Hijāb* is also evident from the incident of Safiyah's (r.a.) wedding to the Prophet (s.a.w.). Anas (r.a.) narrates: The Prophet stayed for three nights between Khaibar and Madīnah and was married to Safiyah. I invited the Muslims to his marriage banquet (*Walīmah*) and there was neither meat nor bread in that banquet but the Prophet ordered Bilāl to spread the leather mats on which dates, dried yogurt and butter were put. The Muslims said amongst themselves, "Will she (i.e. Safiyah) be one of the Mothers of the Believers, (i.e. one of the Wives of the Prophet) or just (a lady captive) of what his right-hand possesses." Some of them said, "If the Prophet makes her observe the *Hijāb*, then she will be one of the Mothers of the Believers (i.e. one of the Prophet's Wives), and if he does not make her observe the *Hijāb*, then she will be his lady slave." So when he departed, he made a place for her behind him (on his camel) and made her observe the *Hijāb*. (*Bukhārī*)

The above Hadīth clearly shows that the Companions of the Prophet (s.a.w.) commonly knew that a free woman was required to observe *Hijāb*. Thus, if he asked her to observe *Hijāb*, she would be his wife; otherwise she would be a slave girl. If *Hijāb* had not become customary by then, the Companions would have never thought of this criteria.

HIJĀB FOR WOMEN SERVANTS

Another thing which should be clearly understood here is that the slave girls or lady captives mentioned in the above Hadīth means, women who get captured as prisoners of war in a battle with unbelievers and are distributed among the soldiers to be looked after. These women become legal slave women. In the present time, there are no such slaves - men or women.

The women who are employed to work as household aids do not fall in the category of women slaves. They are required to observe *Hijāb* in the same way as a free woman.

OBSERVING *HIJĀB* DURING MEDICAL TREATMENT

Hijāb should be observed even during the medical treatment as best as possible. Jābir (r.a.) narrates:

5.

و عن جابر رضي الله عنه ان ام سلمه رضي الله عنها استاذنت رسول الله صلي الله عليه وسلم في الحجامة فامر ابا طيبة ان يحجمها قال حسبت انه كان اخاها من الرضاعة او غلاما لم يحتلم (مسلم)

> Once Ummi Salamah (r.a.) asked permission from the Prophet (s.a.w.) for Cupping (*Hajāmah*)[9]. The Prophet (s.a.w.) asked Abū Taiba to Cup Ummi Salamah. Jābir (r.a.) said: I think the Prophet (s.a.w.) asked Abū Taiba to Cup Ummi Salamah because either he was her foster brother or a young boy. (*Muslim*)

This Hadīth points to the need for *Hijāb* even during medical treatment, because if it was not necessary Jābir (r.a.) would not have clarified that Abū Taiba was Ummi Salamah's foster brother or a young boy.

In this day and age, we see that even in the homes where women observe *Hijāb*, they become quite careless about it when

---

[9] *Hajāmah* (Cupping): The application of a cup shaped instrument to the skin to draw the blood to the surface for bloodletting.

seeking medical treatment. The above Hadīth points out that even for medical treatment, one should attempt to go to a *Mahram* where possible. If one is not available, then a *Ghair-Mahram* may provide treatment as well.

TO UNCOVER *SATR*[10] FOR MEDICAL TREATMENT

It is permissible to uncover *Satr* for the purpose of medical treatment, but only as much as absolutely necessary according to this important principle of *Sharī'ah*: الضرورة تقدر بقدر الضرورة. For example, if the doctor can do with checking the pulse and asking for symptoms, he would not be permitted to touch or see any thing else. Similarly, if there is a wound in the arm or ankle, he may see only that part which is affected. If eyes, nose or mouth need to be examined, only those may be uncovered and not the entire face. These restrictions will also be applicable to a doctor who is *Mahram* for the patient, because even he may not look at the entire body of a *Mahram* woman. She is not permitted to uncover her back, her front, or her thighs even in front of *Mahāram*. Therefore, if the wound is on one of these body parts, the doctor will be permitted to examine only the place of wound regardless of whether he is a *Mahram* or not. This may be accomplished by using old clothes with a hole made at the place of wound. Since a woman is not permitted to uncover any parts of her body between the navel and the knees in front of even other women; therefore, even a lady doctor will be permitted to examine these places only as needed through clothes with openings made at the required places. It should also be remembered that while the doctor is examining the patient, the relatives who are present are not permitted to observe those parts; except for such a person who is lawfully permitted to see those body parts. For example, if the doctor is examining the ankle

---

[10] The whole body of a woman, except the face, the hands and the feet, is *Satr* which is not allowed to be uncovered even before her father, uncle, brother or son, and during *Salāt*.

and if the father or a brother is present, they may observe it as it is not unlawful for a *Mahram* to observe the ankle of a *Mahram* woman.

It should be clearly understood that all the above applies to the medical treatment of men as well, as it is not permitted for men to uncover their body parts between the navel and the knee in front of other men. Therefore, if the doctor needs to examine a man's buttocks or give a shot in the behind, he must only see as much of the body part as is absolutely necessary.

HIJĀB UNDER *IHRĀM*

There is such an emphasis on *Hijāb* in Islamic *Sharī'ah* that even in the state of *Ihrām*, it is necessary to observe *Hijāb*.

6.

عن عائشه رضي الله عنها قالت كان الركبان يمرون بنا
و نحن مع رسول الله صلي الله عليه وسلم محرمات فاذا
حاذوا بنا سدلت احدانا جلبابها من راسها علي وجهها
فاذا جاوزونا كشفناه (ابوداؤد، ج١ ص٢٥)

'Āishah (r.a.) narrated that we were with the Prophet (s.a.w.) in the state of *Ihrām* (during *Hajj*). When men passed by us, we used to pull our shawls down in front of our faces; and when they passed us, we used to lift the shawls up. (*Abū Dāwūd*, vol. 1, p. 254)

Due to a lack of knowledge, many people believe that *Hijāb* is not necessary in the state of *Ihrām* because it is not permissible to have clothes or anything else touch the face while one is in *Ihrām*. Such beliefs are obviously due to their ignorance as it is clear from the above Hadīth that *Hijāb* is necessary even in the state of *Ihrām*. Although there is a slightly different way to observe *Hijāb* during *Ihrām*. For example, wearing a hat with a projected flap around and wearing a veil on top of it in a way that the veil does not touch the face. This is how *Hijāb* is observed by a number of women in the state of *Ihrām*. The Wives of the Prophet (s.a.w.) also covered their faces with their shawls in front of *Ghair-Mahram* during Ihrām.

There is a similar Hadīth narrated by Fātimah Bint Mundir. She stated, "In the state of *Ihrām*, we used to cover our faces with our shawls. Asmah (r.a.), the daughter of Abūbakr Siddīq (r.a.), was also with us and she did not stop us from this." (*Mu'attā Imām Mālik*) That is, she did not say to them that it was forbidden to cover their faces during *Ihrām* and that it was not permissible.

In another Hadīth, 'Āishah (r.a.) narrated that a woman should hang her shawl in front of her face in the state of *Ihrām* (*Fath-ul Bāri*, Book of *Hajj*).

HIJĀB WITH IN-LAWS

People who live in the same household get so close to each other that at times they don't think about the principles of *Sharī'ah*. Therefore, *Hijāb* is often not observed with the brothers-in-law; although there is a strong emphasis on observing *Hijāb* with them.

7.

عن عقبة بن عامر رضي الله عنه قال قال رسول الله
صلي الله عليه وسلم اياكم والدخول علي النساء فقال
رجل يارسول الله ارأيت الحمو قال الحمو الموت
(بخاري، مسلم)

'Uqbah Bin 'Āmir (r.a.) narrates that the Prophet (s.a.w.) once said, "Do not go near *Ghair-Mahram* women." One man asked him, "O Prophet of Allah, what is the Command about the in-laws of a woman?" The Prophet (s.a.w.)

responded, "The (dangers in not observing *Hijāb* with) in-laws are like death (*Bukhārī, Muslim*).

The most noteworthy thing in the above Hadīth is the fact that the Prophet (s.a.w.) compared the men of in-laws to death. This means that a woman should be even more careful in observing *Hijāb* with her brothers-in-law. Although a woman is required to observe *Hijāb* with all *Ghair-Mahram* men, to avoid coming in front of the brothers-in-law without *Hijāb* is as important as it is to avoid death.

The reason for this is that since these men are considered part of the family, they freely enter the ladies quarters and are frequently even invited in, becoming too close which at times results in illegitimate affairs. The poor husband considers them part of his household and does not even think about stopping them from freely mixing with his wife. But, when they come to his house frequently and if the husband is frequently away, all kinds of seemingly impossible things may occur. It is not as easy for a neighbour to kidnap a woman from his neighbour's house as it is easy for a brother-in-law to kidnap or abuse his sister-in-law.

It is because of these reasons that the Prophet (s.a.w.) has strongly advised to strictly observe *Hijāb* with the in-laws and to avoide men among the in-laws as one avoids death. Similarly, men of the in-laws have been instructed not to freely mix with their sisters-in-law and not to look at these women.

MODESTY (*HAYĀ*) AND HONOUR

All the Ahādīth mentioned above were about observing the *Hijāb* - covering the face and the entire body. The Islamic *Sharī'ah* has not stopped at giving the Commandments of *Hijāb*, it has also clarified every such thing which directly relates to these Commandments and, with the slightest carelessness, may result in vulgarity and shamelessness. In other words, many such things have also been forbidden in order to close the doors to indecency and lewdness.

Modesty and maintaining one's honour are of primary importance in preserving the moral fibre of any society. This is why modesty has been called the ornament of a woman, which protects her from many sins and which prevents ill-intentioned men from daring to have bad thoughts about her. This modesty has been made part of her nature to safeguard her from being abused by immoral men.

8.

عن ابن عمر رضي الله عنه عن النبي صلي الله عليه وسلم قال ان الحياء والايمان قرناء جميعا فاذا رفع احدهما رفع الاخر (بيهقي في شعب الايمان)

'Abdullah Bin 'Umar (r.a.) narrated that the Prophet (s.a.w.) said, "Indeed *Hayā* (Modesty) and *Īmān* are Companions. When one of them is lifted, the other leaves as well." (*Baihaqī, Shu'abul Īman*)

In another Hadīth, the Prophet (s.a.w.) has said that *Hayā* is part of *Īmān*. (*Muslim*, vol. 1, p. 47)

Once the Prophet (s.a.w.) saw a man admonishing his brother about *Hayā*. The Prophet said to this man, "Indeed *Hayā* is part of *Īmān*." (Ibid.)

In another Hadīth, the Prophet (s.a.w.) has said, "Only good things result from *Hayā*."

In another Hadīth he has said, "When lewdness is part of any thing, it becomes defective; and when *Hayā* is part of any thing, it becomes beautiful." (*Tirmizī*, vol. 2, p. 122)

In one Hadīth, the Prophet (s.a.w.) said, "*Hayā* and trustworthiness will be the first things to go from this world; therefore, keep asking Allah for them." (*Baihaqī, Firdaus Al-Dailmī*)

The truth is that *Hayā* is a special characteristic of a Mu'min.[11] People who are ignorant of the teachings of the Prophet (s.a.w.) do not concern themselves with *Hayā* and Honour. *Hayā* and *Īmān* are interdependent; therefore, either they both exist together or they both perish. Thus, the Prophet (s.a.w.) has said in one Hadīth, "When there is no *Hayā* left in you, then do as you please."

Today, vulgarity and all its ingredients have become common place even among well-known Muslims in the zeal of imitating the non-believers. It is these people who have been struggling to bring Muslim women out of *Hijāb* into immodesty and indecency. They have adopted the lifestyle of the Christians more than the traditions of the Prophet (s.a.w.). Such people are in a dilemma. On the one hand, they desire to freely look at the half-clad bodies of the Wives and daughters of other Muslims on the streets; and on the other hand, they do not have the courage to deny the teachings of the Holy Qur'ān and Ahādīth. Neither can they say that they have given up Islam, nor can they bear to see Muslim women observing *Hijāb*. Actually, indulging in indecency for a long time has killed their sense of honour and modesty which Islam has commanded to preserve. It is this natural desire of maintaining one's honour which compels men to protect the respect and honour of their women.

9.

عن مالك بن احيمر رضي الله عنه قال سمعت رسول الله
صلى الله عليه وسلم لا يقبل الله من الصقور يوم القيمة
صرفا ولا عدلا قلنا يارسول الله و ماالصقور قال الذي

---

[11] A faithful Muslim who practices his Faith.

يدخل علي اهله الرجال
(كشف الاستار عن زوائدالبرار، ص١٨٧)

> Mālik Bin Uhaimir reported that he heard the Prophet (s.a.w.) saying that Allah (s.w.t.) will not accept any good deeds or worship of an immodest and vulgar person. We asked, "O Prophet of Allah! Who is immodest and vulgar?" He replied, "A man whose wife entertains *Ghair-Mahram* men." (*Kashf-ul Astār 'An Zawāid-ul Barār*, p. 187)

In another Hadīth, the Prophet (s.a.w.) has said, "There are three people who will neither go to the Heaven nor will smell even the fragrance of it: first, a man who adopts the appearance of a woman; second, an alcoholic; and third, a *Dayyūs*." People asked, "O Prophet of Allah! Who is a *Dayyūs*?" He replied, "One who tolerates indecency and immorality in his woman." In another narration, his reply has been worded, "One who does not maintain honour and decency in his wife." (*Tafsīr Āyāt-ul Ahkām*, vol. 2, p. 167)

In yet another narration his reply was: *Dayyūs* is a person who does not care who is visiting his wife. (*Tabrānī, Jam'ul Fawāid*, vol. 1, p. 400)

In one Hadīth, it has been said that no one has a better sense of honour than Allah which is why he has forbidden lewdness. (*Bukhārī*)

Once Sa'd Bin 'Ubādah (r.a.) said, "I will not hesitate killing my wife with my sword if I see her with a strange man." The Prophet (s.a.w.) said to the audience, "Are you surprised at Sa'd's sense of honour? I have a higher sense of honour than Sa'd and Allah has it even higher than me."

In another Hadīth, the Prophet (s.a.w.) has said, "I have a sense of honour. Only a person with a darkened heart is deprived of a sense of honour." (*Ihyā 'Ulūm Al-Dīn*) This is to say that a person's exceeding indulgence in indecency results in a loss of wisdom and the ability to differentiate between good and bad.

TO GO OUT WITHOUT NECESSITY

With respect to societal purity and *Hijāb*, the Islamic *Sharī'ah* also commands that women should not leave their homes without necessity to reduce the probability of getting into mischief (*Fitnah*).

10.

عن ابن عمر رضي الله عنه عن رسول الله صلي الله عليه
وسلم قال المرأة عورة فانها اذا خرجت
استشرفهاالشيطان وانها لا تكون اقرب الي الله منها في
قعر بيتها (طبراني)

> Ibn 'Umar (r.a.) quoted the Prophet (s.a.w.) as saying, "Women are to be kept in hiding. Indeed when she leaves her home, Shaitān keeps an eye on her. Certainly a woman is closest to Allah when she is in her home." (*Tabrānī*)

Truly, a woman is safe from all the mischief until she stays in her home. When she steps out of her home without necessity, she is highly capable of becoming a tool of Shaitān. This is why it has been said in one Hadīth that when a woman comes in front of a *Ghair-Mahram*, she comes in the guise of Shaitān. (*Abū Dāwūd*, vol. 1, p. 292)

In another Hadīth, Mu'āz (r.a.) reported the Prophet (s.a.w.) as saying: Protect yourselves from the mischief of women, because Iblīs[12] is a very wise hunter; he hunts very successfully through women. (*Firdaus Al-Dailmī, Mirqāt*, vol. 6, p. 190)

In one Hadīth, the Prophet (s.a.w.) said, "For men, I have not found any mischief (*Fitnah*) more harmful than women." (*Bukhārī, Muslim*)

In another Hadīth, he said, "This world is sweet and attractive, and Allah has made you His deputy here. He watches over you to see how you conduct yourselves. You should protect yourself from the love of this world and from the mischief (*Fitnah*) of women, because the very first mischief in Banī Isrāīl was caused through women."

It is a necessary condition for women, in order to preserve their modesty and honour, that they stay in their homes and not step out unnecessarily for fun and to roam around in the market place.

Ali (r.a.) narrates that once the Prophet (s.a.w.) asked the Companions, "What is the best thing for a woman?" Nobody answered. Later when I went home, I asked Fātimah the same question. She replied, "The best thing for a woman is to protect herself from the eyes of men." I told the Prophet (s.a.w.) Fātimah's answer. He replied, "Indeed, Fātimah is a part of me." (*Kashf-ul Astār*, p. 150)

In another Hadīth, the Prophet (s.a.w.) has said, "The best deed of the women of my *Ummah* is contentment and withdrawal from men." (*Shara'ī Hijāb*, p. 30)

There is so much emphasis placed on women to stay in their homes that their open participation in the important worship

---

[12] A name of Shaitan.

like *Salāt* and necessities like funerals and burials is not considered desirable.

OFFERING *SALĀT* AT HOME

As it has been mentioned previously, it is permissible for women to come out of their homes when necessary. And, since *Salāt* is a necessity, it is permissible for them to go to the Masjid (mosque) provided that they cover themselves properly and do not wear perfume and noisy ornaments. In spite of this permission, the Prophet (s.a.w.) pronounced that it is better for them to offer their *Salāt* at home.

11.

عن عبدالله بن مسعود رضي الله عنه عن النبي صلي الله عليه وسلم قال صلوةالمرأة في بيتها افضل من صلوتها في حجرتها و صلوتها في مخدعها افضل من صلوتها في بيتها (ابوداؤد، ج١ ص٨)

'Abdullah Bin Mas'ūd (r.a.) narrated that the Prophet (s.a.w.) said, "It is better for a woman to offer her *Salāt* in her bedroom than in the living room; and it is better for her to offer her *Salāt* in her living room than in her courtyard." (*Abū Dāwūd*, vol. 1, p. 84)

In another Hadīth, Ummi Salamah (r.a.) has reported the Prophet (s.a.w.) as saying: the best Masājid (mosques) for women are the innermost rooms of their houses. (*Musnad Ahmad*)

In one Hadīth, the Prophet (s.a.w.) said, "The most likeable *Salāt* of a woman to Allah is the one which she offers in her house privately and in a dark place." (*Ibn Khuzaimah*)

Ibn 'Umar (r.a.) narrated this saying of the Prophet (s.a.w.): "A woman's *Salāt* which is offered in her privacy is 25 times better than her *Salāt* with congregation." (*Kanz Al-Ummāl*)

This has been exaggerated to the point that it was said that for a woman offering her *Salāt* at home is even better than offering in Masjid-al-Harām and Masjid-al-Nabawī where offering one *Salāt* is better than offering 100,000 *Salāts* and 50,000 *Salāts* respectively. Therefore, in Ahādīth we find a story of a female Companion of the Prophet (s.a.w.), Ummi Sa'dia (r.a.), who came to the Prophet (s.a.w.) and said, "O Prophet of Allah! I wish to offer my *Salāt* with you in congregation in the Masjid (mosque)." The Prophet (s.a.w.) replied, "I know how much you desire to offer your *Salāt* behind me in congregation, but offering the *Salāt* in the innermost part of your house is better than offering it in the living room, and offering *Salāt* in the living room is better than offering it in your courtyard, and offering *Salāt* in the courtyard is better than offering it in your neighbourhood Masjid (mosque), and offering your *Salāt* in the neighbourhood Masjid (mosque) is better than coming to my Masjid (mosque)." (*Musnad Ahmad*). In *Ibn Khuzaimah*, this narration also includes the statement that after Ummi Sa'dia heard the Prophet (s.a.w.), she set aside a place in the innermost and darkest corner of her house for *Salāt* and offered her *Salāt* there as long as she lived.

'Urwah (r.a.) narrated this saying of 'Āishah (r.a.): The women of Banī Isrāīl used to make wooden sandals which they wore to their places of worship, and they used to provide attractions for men; so, Allah forbade them to go to the Masjid (mosque). (*Musnad Abdur Razzāq*)

In another Hadīth, we find this saying of 'Āishah (r.a.): If the Prophet (s.a.w.) would have seen the attitude of women which they adopted after him, he would have surely stopped them from coming to the Masjid (mosque) as the women of Banī Isrāīl were stopped. (*Muslim*)

PARTICIPATION IN *JIHĀD*

The best of the worships is to sacrifice one's life in the path of Allah. However, Islamic *Sharī'ah* has not preferred participation of women even in *Jihād*, as they may earn the rewards of *Jihād* without actually participating in it.

12.

عن انس رضي الله عنه قال جئن النساء الي رسول الله صلي الله عليه وسلم فقلن يارسول الله ذهب الرجال بالفضل والجهاد في سبيل الله فما لنا عمل ندرك به عمل المجاهدين في سبيل الله فقال رسول الله صلي الله عليه وسلم من قعدت منكن في بيتها فانها تدرك عمل المجاهدين في سبيل الله (مسند بزار)

Anas (r.a.) reported that once a group of women came to the Prophet (s.a.w.) and said, "O Prophet of Allah! Men have reaped all the rewards of participating in *Jihād*; show us a deed which would help us reach the rewards of the *Mujāhidīn*." The Prophet (s.a.w.) replied, "Any one of you who stays in her home protecting her modesty and honour will receive the rewards of *Jihād*." (*Musnad Bazzār*)

Once 'Āishah (r.a.) asked the Prophet (s.a.w.), "O Prophet of Allah! we consider *Jihād* the best of the deeds; should we not participate in it as well?" He replied, "Women's *Jihād* is to go for *Hajj* (Pilgrimage)." (*Bukhārī*)

In another Hadīth, Abū Qatādah (r.a.) has reported the Prophet (s.a.w.) as saying: *Jihād*, Friday prayer, and going to the cemetery for burials are not required of women. (*Tabrānī*)

ETIQUETTES OF EMERGING FROM HOME

From the above Ahādīth, it is sufficiently clear that Islamic *Sharī'ah* wants women to emerge from their homes as little as possible. The *Sharī'ah* provides a number of etiquettes for when they need to come out. Among these, *Hijāb* and covering of face have been covered in detail previously.

THE USE OF PERFUME AND ORNAMENTS: An important etiquette is not to come out wearing fragrance and ornaments.

13.

عن ميمونه بنت سعد رضي الله عنها و كانت خادمةالنبي صلي الله عليه وسلم قالت قال رسول الله صلي الله عليه وسلم مثل الرافلة في الزينة في غير اهلها كمثل ظلمة يوم القيمة لا نور لها

> Maimūnah Bint Sa'd (r.a.), who was one of the Prophet's servants, reported him as saying: "A woman who decorates herself for anyone else other than her husband is like such a darkness in the Day of Judgement which has no light in it."

The women who decorate themselves, freely participate in parties with men, and are considered these days the life of the parties, have been pronounced as the darkness of the parties by the Prophet (s.a.w.).

In another Hadīth, Maimūnah Bint Sa'd narrated that the Prophet (s.a.w.) said, "Allah remains displeased with a woman who emerges from her home wearing perfume and gives men the opportunity to look at her, until she returns home." (*Tabrānī*)

The Prophet (ṣ.a.w.) has also said, "A woman who passes by men wearing perfume so that they will be entertained, is committing adultery; and so are those eyes who look upon her. (*Nasāī, Ibn Khuzaimah*)

'Āishah (r.a.) narrated that once a woman of the Muzainah tribe came to the Prophet (s.a.w.) in the Masjid (mosque). She was dressed fashionably and was walking with dalliance. The Prophet (s.a.w.) said to the audience, "O people! Stop your women from dressing fashionably and from walking in the Masjid (mosque) with dalliance. Because, Banī Israīl were not condemned until their women began to decorate themselves and come to their Masjid (mosque) walking with dalliance." (*Ibn Mājah*)

Abū Hurairah (r.a.) reported that once I saw a woman who was wearing very strong perfume and a tight dress. I asked her, "O servant of Allah, are you coming from the Masjid (mosque)?" She said, "Yes." He said to her, "I have heard my beloved Abul Qāsim (s.a.w.) saying, 'Allah does not accept the *Salāt* of a woman who comes to pray wearing perfume, until she goes home and takes a bath as she does after coition.'" (*Abū Dāwūd*, vol. 2, p. 219)

EMERGING FROM HOME WITHOUT HUSBAND'S PERMISSION: It is also one of the etiquette for women not to leave their homes without the permission of their husbands.

14.

عن معاذ رضي الله عنه قال قال رسول الله صلي الله عليه وسلم لا يحل لامرأة تومن بالله واليوم الاخر ان تاذن في بيت زوجها إلا بإذنه ولا تخرج و هو كاره ولا تطيع فيه احدا (مستدرك حاكم، طبراني)

Mu'āz (r.a.) narrates that the Prophet (s.a.w.) has said, "It is not permissible for any woman who believes in Allah and the Day of Judgement to allow anyone to enter her husband's house, or to leave home without her husband's permission; and that she should not obey anyone else in this regard." (*Mustadrak Al-Hākim, Tabrānī*)

The principle of asking the husband's permission to go out greatly assists a woman to maintain her honour and virtue. Women who go out wherever they want and invite into their homes whomever they want without their husband's permission, are more likely to lose their honour and character ending up deeper and deeper in a life of sin.

Anas (r.a.) reported the Prophet (s.a.w.) as saying: "Any woman who leaves home without her husband's permission, Allah remains displeased with her until she returns home, or until her husband is pleased with her." (*Kanz Al-Ummāl*)

In another Hadīth narrated by 'Umar (r.a.), we find that the Prophet (s.a.w.) said, "Women should not talk to *Ghair-Mahram* men without their husband's permission." (*Tabrānī*)

TRAVELLING ALONE: To protect the honour of women, the *Sharī'ah* has commanded women to be accompanied by *Mahārim* men when they are travelling, so that they can be protected from mischiefs.

15.

عن ابي سعيد رضي الله عنه ان النبي صلي الله عليه وسلم قال لا يحل لامرأة تومن بالله واليوم الاخر ان تسافر سفرا فوق ثلاثة ايام فصاعدا إلا و معها ابوها او اخوها او زوجها او ابنها او ذومحرم منها

(ابوداؤد، ترمذي، ابن ماجه)

Abū Sa'īd Khudrī (r.a.) reported that the Prophet (s.a.w.) said, "Any woman who believes in Allah and the Day of Judgement should not travel alone for three days or more except when accompanied by her father, brother, husband, son or any other *Mahram* man." (*Abū Dāwūd, Tirmizī, Ibn Mājah*)

The limit of three days, in *Sharī'ah*, signifies any travel where it becomes permissible to offer Qasr *Salāt*.

Ibn 'Abbās (r.a.) narrated that the Prophet (s.a.w.) said, "No man should be with any woman alone, nor should a woman travel without a *Mahram*." One man, who heard this, got up and said, "O Prophet of Allah! I have been enlisted in the army to go to such and such battles, but my wife has left for *Hajj*." The Prophet (s.a.w.) replied, "Go and perform *Hajj* with your wife." (*Bukhārī*)

WALKING ON THE STREET: One of the etiquettes for women to emerge from their homes is for them to walk separately from men. The best way to achieve it is to walk on the side of the street.

16.

عن ابي اسيدالانصاري رضي الله عنه انه سمع رسول الله صلي الله عليه وسلم يقول و هو خارج من المسجد فاختلط الرجال مع النساء في الطريق فقال للنساء استاخرن فانه ليس لكن ان تحققن الطريق عليكن بحافات الطريق فكانت المرأة تلصق بالجدار حتي ان صوبها ليتعلق بالجدار (ابوداؤد، بيهقي)

Abū Usaid Ansārī (r.a.) reported that once the Prophet (s.a.w.) came out of the Masjid (mosque). On the street men and women were walking very close together. When he saw this, he said, "O women! Get in the back. You should walk on the side of the street rather than in the middle." (*Abū Dāwūd, Baihaqī*)

The narrator reported that afterwards the women became so careful about walking on the sides of the streets that their clothes rubbed against the walls on the sides of the streets.[13]

'Abdullah Bin 'Umar (r.a.) narrated that the Prophet (s.a.w.) said, "It is not permissible for women to emerge from their homes except in dire necessity; and they should not walk on the street except on the sides." (*Tabrānī*)

Anas Bin Mālik (r.a.) narrated that the Prophet (s.a.w.) was once going somewhere. In the street, there was a woman walking in front of him. He asked her to walk on a side. She replied, "The road is quite wide." The Companions of the Prophet became quite annoyed. He said to them, "Leave her alone; she is a rebel." (*Jāmi-'ul Usūl*, vol. 6, p. 660)

In another Hadīth, 'Abdullah Bin 'Umar (r.a.) narrated that the Prophet (s.a.w.) prohibited a man to walk between two women. (*Abū Dāwūd*)

GUARDING THE EYES

To create a virtuous society and to protect it from sexual anarchy, the *Sharī'ah*, among other things, has commanded to safeguard the eyes. This is because the eyes serve as a messenger. Not guarding the eyes is the first sign of moral decay.

17.

عن عبدالله بن مسعود رضي الله عنه قال قال رسول الله
صلي الله عليه وسلم الأثم حوازالقلوب و مامن نظرة
للشيطان فيها مطمع (بيهقي)

[13] In those days, the streets were narrow with houses on both sides.

'Abdullah Bin Mas'ūd narrated that the Prophet (s.a.w.) said, "The desires and the sins sway the hearts; and Shaitān has high expectations of the eye which is raised to look at a *Ghair-Mahram*." (*Baihaqī*)

In one Hadīth Qudsī, the Prophet (s.a.w.) reported that Allah says, "Looking at a *Ghair-Mahram* is one of the poisoned arrows of Shaitān. Whosoever will stop it (looking at *Ghair-Mahram*) because of fearing me, I will bless him with such *Īmān*, the sweetness of which he will feel in his heart." (*Tabrānī, Mustadrak Al-Hākim*) This also means that as a punishment of looking at *Ghair-Mahram*, Allah takes away the sweetness of *Īmān* from a Mu'min.

In another Hadīth, the Prophet (s.a.w.) has said, "On the Day of Judgement, molten lead will be dropped in the eyes of a person who lustfully looks at a woman's beauty." (*Az-Zawājir*)

The Prophet (s.a.w.) has said in one Hadīth, "Lower your gaze and protect your honour; otherwise, your faces will be darkened." (*Tabrānī*)

In one Hadīth, he said, "Don't sit and wait on the roadside; and if you must, then protect your eyes from looking at the *Ghair-Mahram* passing by." (*Muslim*)

To safeguard one's eyes and the effort it takes to control one's desires (*Nafs*) is an on-going good deed which the Prophet (s.a.w.) has encouraged in many different ways. For example, he said, "There are three kinds of men whose eyes will not see the hell-fire. One, the eye which is busy watching the enemy during *Jihād* in the path of Allah; second, the eye which cries with the fear of Allah; and third, the eye which is held from looking at what Allah has forbidden." (*Majma'uz-Zawāid*)

In another Hadīth, the Prophet (s.a.w.) said, "A Muslim who accidently looks at the beauty of a woman and, instead of continuing to look at her, lowers his gaze will be rewarded by Allah with such worship, the sweetness of which he will clearly feel." (*Musnad Ahmad*)

The Prophet (s.a.w.) has also said, "If you guarantee me six things, I will guarantee Paradise for you: 1) When you speak, do not lie; 2) Do not breach your trust; 3) Do not break a promise; 4) Lower your gaze; 5) Protect your hands from oppression; and 6) Guard your honour." (*Musnad Ahmad*, vol. 5, p. 323)

In one Hadīth, the Prophet (s.a.w.) said, "Be very clear that Allah curses the person who looks at *Ghair-Mahram* and exhibits himself/herself in front of them." (*Mishkāt*, p. 270)

This Hadīth provides a lot of other details. In principle, it denounces all forbidden gazes. It not only condemns the person who is gazing but also the one who is willfully showing off himself or herself. A person who opens any such part of his/her body, which is not permissible to look at by others, and the one who looks at it, both deserve to be cursed.

WILFULLY GOING TO A PLACE WHERE *HIJĀB* IS NOT BEING OBSERVED: In the interpretation of the above Hadīth, the following circumstances are also included where men and women would deserve to be cursed by Allah.

Any woman who goes out to the market place or any other public place without *Hijāb* and the *Ghair-Mahram* men who gaze at her.

A woman who stands in her balcony, window or sun deck without *Hijāb* where she can see and be seen by *Ghair-Mahram* men.

In weddings, the bridegroom who goes in the ladies section, where he can see and be seen by *Ghair-Mahram* women.

A woman who uncovers any part of her body between the navel and just below the knees in front of another woman. Similarly, a man who uncovers these parts of his body in front of another man.

A woman who uncovers any part of her body in front of her *Mahāram*, such as her father, brother, etc. Today in many westernized homes, women, following the footsteps of their western sisters, wear short dresses with underwears which leaves their thighs and legs visible to all men in the home including the male servants (who, by the way, should not be allowed to come in the ladies quarters). Thus, all men and women of the household become deserving of the curse by Allah.

Lastly, it should be understood about *Ghadd Al-Basar* (guarding the eyes) that it is not permissible to intentionally look at *Ghair-Mahram*, but if one unintentionally looked at one, he/she should not continue to stare or to have a second look. Thus, we find in a Hadīth narrated by Jarīr Bin 'Abdullah Bajalī (r.a.) that he asked the Prophet (s.a.w.) about the sudden and unintentional glimpse (at a *Ghair-Mahram*). He replied, "Turn your eyes away." (*Muslim*, *Tirmizī*) In another Hadīth, the Prophet (s.a.w.) said to Ali (r.a.), "O Ali! You have a large share in the Paradise. Do not look at a *Ghair-Mahram* again after the first unintentional look. The unintentional look is forgiven." (*Musnad Bazzār*)

BEING ALONE WITH *GHAIR-MAHRAM* MAN

When a *Ghair-Mahram* man and woman live together or meet in privacy, it often results in illegitimate and immoral conduct. This is why the *Sharī'ah* has forbidden it to prevent corruption.

18.

وعن عمر رضي الله عنه عن النبي صلي الله عليه وسلم
قال لا يخلون رجل بامرأة ألا كان ثالثهما الشيطان
(ترمذي)

> 'Umar (r.a.) narrated that the Prophet (s.a.w.) said, When a *Ghair-Mahram* man and woman meet in privacy, the third one present is Shaitān. (*Tirmizī*)

We know that Shaitān's job is to lead people astray. When a man and woman are meeting together in privacy, he is there to emotionally excite them and to invite them to engage in unbecoming conduct. This is why the Prophet (s.a.w.) has prohibited it. It is necessary to emphatically follow this prohibition. Even elders, teachers, mentors, and cousins should strongly avoid being with *Ghair-Mahram* in privacy. Doing so is sinful.

'Amr Bin Al-'Ās (r.a.) narrated that the Prophet (s.a.w.) prohibited them to visit women without their husband's permission.[14]

In another Hadīth, the Prophet (s.a.w.) said, "Do not visit women in the absence of their husbands because Shaitān circulates inside you like your blood." (*Tirmizī*)

In one Hadīth, the Prophet (s.a.w.) said, "After today, nobody should visit any woman in the absence of her husband unless he is accompanied by a few other men."

---

[14] These Ahādīth pertain to the circumstances which necessitate *Ghair-Mahram* men visiting women. Under all such circumstances, *Hijāb* must be observed.

The Prophet (s.a.w.) has also said, "Do not visit the Wives of *Mujāhidīn* while they are away from their homes." (*Kashf-ul Astār*, p. 216)

Jābir (r.a.) narrated a Hadīth where the Prophet (s.a.w.) said, "Beware, no one should spend a night alone in a house with a single (divorced or widowed) woman unless he is married to her, or happens to be her *Mahram*." (*Muslim*)

In the above Hadīth, it is prohibited for any man to spend a night alone in a house with a *Ghair-Mahram* woman. This prohibition is based on foresight and wisdom. In principle, it is prohibited for a *Ghair-Mahram* man and woman to be alone together under all circumstances, but the specific prohibition of spending a night alone under one roof has been separately mentioned, because in the darkness of night where others are not likely to witness any thing, the opportunities for misconduct are greater. Again, all the *Ghair-Mahram* relatives, such as cousins and brothers-in-law, are also included in this prohibition. Often, women do not take precaution with these men and go in front of them without *Hijāb* unhesitantly. This prohibition is both for men and women. Men have been addressed in the Hadīth, because they are stronger and may not be easily deterred by a woman.

'Allāmah Nawawī writes in the *Sharah Muslim* that the reason why divorced and widowed women were separately mentioned in this Hadīth is that due to being alone, these women become easy prey for men who are looking to marry or have bad intentions otherwise. They will not dare to visit single girls because they protect themselves and are also protected by their parents.

BATHING IN PUBLIC SHOWERS

Among the Commandments provided to safeguard the honour and purity of women, an important one is for them not to take showers or bath in public showers.

19.

عن جابر رضي الله عنه ان النبي صلي الله عليه وسلم قال من كان يومن بالله واليوم الاخر فلا يدخل الحمام بغير ازار و من كان يومن بالله واليوم الاخر فلا يدخل حليلته الحمام و من كان يومن بالله واليوم الاخر فلا يجلس علي مائدة تدار عليه الخمر (ترمذي، نسائ)

Jābir (r.a.) narrates that the Prophet (s.a.w.) said, "Whosoever believes in Allah and the Day of Judgement should not enter a public shower without covering his *Satr*; and whosoever believes in Allah and the Day of Judgement should not take his wife into a public shower; and whosoever believes in Allah and the Day of Judgement should not sit in a place where people are drinking wine." (*Tirmizī*, *Nasāī*)

'Āishah (r.a.) reported that the Prophet (s.a.w.) had forbidden both men and women to enter public showers. Later, he granted permission to men with the condition that they would enter a public shower covering their *Satr*.

In another Hadīth, Ummi Dardā (r.a.) reported that once she met the Prophet (s.a.w.) when she was returning after taking a bath in a public shower. He asked me, "O Ummi Dardā! Where are you coming from?" I replied, "From the public shower." He said, "I swear by the One who has my life in His Hand, any woman who takes off her clothes anywhere else but her home, disgraces herself with Allah." (*Musnad Ahmad*, vol. 6, p. 362)

Qārī Mohammed Tayyab writes in his book *Shara'ī Purdah*: Are the public showers in hotels, clubs, gyms, swimming pools, parks and schools today any better than those public bathing facilities in the olden days? Girls are regularly sent to these places without any protection of their elders resulting in many unfortunate incidents. Is it not a mirror image of (women) displaying themselves in the Days of Ignorance (before Islam), which is strictly forbidden in Qur'ān?

LOOKING AT MEN

As men have been commanded not to look at *Ghair-Mahram* women, similarly women have been asked to abstain from looking at *Ghair-Mahram* men.

20.

وعن ام سلمه رضي الله عنها قالت انها كانت عند رسول الله صلي الله عليه وسلم و ميمونه اذ اقبل ابن ام مكتوم فدخل عليه فقال رسول الله صلي الله عليه وسلم احتجبا منه فقلت يارسول الله اليس هو اعمي لا يبصرنا فقال رسول الله صلي الله عليه وسلم افعمياوان انتماالستما تبصرانه (احمد، ترمذي، ابوداؤد)

Ummul Mu'minīn Salamah (r.a.) reports: Once I and Maimūnah were with the Prophet (s.a.w.) when suddenly 'Abdullah Bin Ummi Maktūm entered the house. Knowing that 'Abdullah was blind, we did not observe *Hijāb* and continued to sit there. The Prophet (s.a.w.) said, "Observe the *Hijāb* in front of him." I asked, "O Prophet of Allah! Isn't he blind? He can't see us." He replied, "Are both of you blind as well? Can't you see him?" (*Ahmad*, *Tirmizī*, *Abū Dāwūd*)

It is clear from the above Hadīth that women should not look at men as much as possible, as has also been mentioned in the Holy Qur'ān: "Say to the believing women to lower their gaze....." (*Sūrah Nūr*, v. 30). 'Abdullah (r.a.) was a blind and very pious Companion of the Prophet (s.a.w.), and both the Wives of the Prophet (s.a.w.) were very pious as well. In spite of this, the Prophet (s.a.w.) asked them to observe *Hijāb* in front of him.

ADOPTING THE WAYS OF THE OPPOSITE SEX

In order to prevent sexual corruption and moral anarchy, the Islamic *Sharī'ah* has given separate and specific Commands to men and women for governing themselves which are sensible and in harmony with their nature.

21.

و عن ابن ابي مليكة رضي الله عنه قال قيل لعائشه رضي الله عنها ان امرأة تلبس النعل قالت لعن رسول الله عليه الرجلة من النساء (ابوداؤد، ج٢ ص٢١٠)

> Ibn Abī Mulaikah (r.a.) reported that once somebody asked 'Āishah (r.a.) about a woman who used to wear men's shoes. 'Āishah (r.a.) replied, "The Prophet of Allah has cursed a woman who adopts the ways of men." (*Abū Dāwūd*, vol. 2, p. 210)

Tamīm Dārī (r.a.) narrated that he heard the Prophet (s.a.w.) prohibiting women from wearing men's hats and shoes as well as from going to men's gatherings and from wearing men's trousers and shirts. (*Kashfun Ni'mah*, vol. 1, p. 163)

Abū Hurairah (r.a.) reported that once an eunuch, who had coloured his hands and feet with henna, was brought to the Prophet (s.a.w.). The Prophet asked who this person was. People told him that he imitates women. The Prophet (s.a.w.) ordered that he be exiled from Madīnah. (*Abū Dāwūd*)

Ibn 'Abbās (r.a.) narrated that the Prophet (s.a.w.) cursed the men who adopt the looks of women, and the women who adopt the ways of men; and that he asked us to throw them out of our homes. (*Bukhārī*)

It is clear from the above Ahādīth that the Prophet (s.a.w.) utterly disliked men who wear ladies' clothes and behave effeminately as well as women who wear men's clothes and behave like men.

It also does not make any sense for men to look and behave like women or vice versa. But today, we choose not to follow the advice of our beloved Prophet (s.a.w.). Instead, we follow the models provided to us by Europe and America's non-believers. We blindly adopt their fashions and dresses and, in doing so, consider ourselves modernized and respectable, even if such behaviour brings us the curse and displeasure of Allah. May Allah give us the wisdom and courage to follow the Guidance of His beloved Prophet (s.a.w.). Whatever Allah and His Prophet (s.a.w.) have given us is entirely for our own benefit.

COMMANDMENTS ABOUT DRESS

It seems proper at this point to briefly explain the Commandments of *Sharī'ah* about the dress for men and women, and to show how undesirable nudity is in Islam, for this matter is also related to *Hijāb*.

It is required in *Sharī'ah* for men and women to cover those parts of the body which are known as *Satr*. After *Īmān*, the first obligation on a Muslim is to cover these parts of his/her body. This has been an obligation since the beginning of man and it has been an obligation in the *Sharī'ah* of all the Prophets. Even before the man was sent to this earth, when Allah took away the dress of Paradise from Adam (a.s.) and Hawwa (a.s.) as a result of disobeying Allah's Command not to taste the fruit of the forbidden tree, both of them covered their *Satr* with leaves. Thus, it even seems to be a part of human nature and instinct to cover the private parts of his/her body.

In the *Sharī'ah* of all the Prophets, from Adam (a.s.) to Hadhrat Muhammad Mustafā (s.a.w.), it has been obligatory to cover the *Satr*. There might have been minor differences in the limits and determination of the parts that must be covered, but it is universally accepted that covering certain parts of the body has been a part of the *Sharī'ah* of all the Prophets. Each man and woman is obliged to follow this Command regardless of whether somebody is watching him/her or not. Thus, if a person is offering his/her prayers in the nude on a dark night where there is no one to watch him, his/her prayer has been declared unanimously unacceptable by the jurists. Similarly, if one is offering his/her prayer in a place where nobody is watching him and if his/her *Satr* becomes exposed during the prayer, the prayer becomes invalid.

PROHIBITION OF NUDITY AND REQUIREMENT OF *SATR*: Allah has pronounced clothes as a blessing in the Holy Qur'ān, and has clearly stated that they serve the purpose of covering those parts of human body which a person instinctively considers wrong to expose. Nudity has been considered derogatory in many Ahādīth as well.

22.

عن ابن عمر رضي الله عنه ان رسول الله صلي الله عليه وسلم قال اياكم والتعري فان معكم من لا يفارقكم إلا عندالغائط و حين يفضي الرجال الي اهله فاستحيوهم و اكرموهم (ترمذي)

Ibn 'Umar (r.a.) narrated that the Prophet (s.a.w.) said, "Save yourself from nudity because two angles are with you all the time, except when you go to the toilet or engage in sexual intercourse; so, be bashful of them and respect their presence." (*Tirmizī*)

In one Hadīth, the Prophet (s.a.w.) has said, "I prefer falling from the sky and breaking into pieces than to look at anybody's *Satr* or to have somebody look at mine." (*Mabsūt Sarkhasī*)

Abū Sa'īd Khudrī (r.a.) narrated that the Prophet (s.a.w.) said, "No man should look at the *Satr* of another man and no woman should look at the *Satr* of another woman. Also, no man should be with another man under one piece of cloth and no woman should be with another woman under one piece of cloth." (*Muslim*)

Bahz Bin Hakīm (r.a.) narrated that his grandfather once asked the Prophet (s.a.w.), "O Prophet of Allah! With whom should we observe the *Satr*?" He replied, "Protect your *Satr* from everyone except your wife and your slave-women." I asked, "O Prophet of Allah! Sometimes a person is alone." He replied, "Allah is more deserving of bashfulness from you." (*Tirmizī*)

Ibn 'Abbās (r.a.) reported that he was told (by the Prophet) not to walk around naked exposing the *Satr*. (*Az-Zawājir*)

Once the Prophet (s.a.w.) passed by the grazing place of camels which were given as *Sadaqah*. He saw the shepherd lying naked in the sun. The Prophet (s.a.w.) immediately dismissed him and said, "No shameless person should work for us." (*Mabsūt Sarkhasī*)

Once the Prophet (s.a.w.) was going somewhere when he saw a servant publicly taking a bath in nude. He said to him, "I don't find you bashful with Allah. Consider yourself dismissed. We don't need your service." (*Az-Zawājir*)

Nudity has been denounced to the extent that a husband and wife, even while having intercourse, have been asked to observe the etiquette of *Satr* and not to be completely naked like donkeys. (*Ibn Mājah*)

It should be kept in mind that *Satr* for a man begins from his navel to just below his knees, while the entire body of a woman with the exception of her face, palms and feet are included in *Satr* in front of a man, and from her navel to just below her knees in front of another woman.

CLOTHING: The *Sharī'ah* has not determined a specific type of clothing to be worn by all. People may choose their clothes depending upon the climatic conditions and other needs. However, the important etiquettes Islam has given us about the code of dressing are as follows.

a. The clothes should cover the *Satr* completely.

b. They should not be made of such materials through which the body may be seen.

c. They should not be so tight fitting that the shape of the body is exposed. Such tight clothes, instead of covering the *Satr* and maintaining self-dignity, serve more to show off the body and provide sexual excitement.

d. Men should not wear clothes made out of silk.

e. Men and women should not wear clothes of the opposite sex.

TIGHT AND SEE THROUGH CLOTHES: If the dress is made of such materials through which the body may be seen, it is often more exciting than total nudity. This is why wearing clothes made of such materials have been prohibited.

23.

عن اسامه بن زيد رضي الله عنه قال كساني رسول الله صلي الله عليه وسلم قبطية كشيفة كانت مما اهدي له دحيه الكلبي فكسوتها إمرأتي فقال رسول الله صلي الله عليه وسلم مالك لا تلبس القبطيه فقلت يارسول الله كسوتها إمرأتي فقال مرها ان تجعل تحتها غلالة فاني اخاف ان تصف حجم عظامها (مسند احمد، بزار)

Usāmah Bin Zaid (r.a.) narrated: The Prophet (s.a.w.) gave me a relatively thick piece of material known as *Qibtiyah* which was presented to him by Dahyah Kalabī. I gave that material to my wife. The Prophet (s.a.w.) asked me, "How come you did not wear the *Qibtiyah*?" I replied, "O Prophet of Allah! I gave it to my wife for her dress." He said, "Ask her to make a lining for it; I am afraid (because of being quite thin) it may not cover the frame of her body." (*Musnad Ahmad*, *Bazzār*)

'Āishah (r.a.) narrated: Once my sister Asma came to visit me. She was wearing a dress made of some thin Syrian material which you now call *Saffak.* When the Prophet (s.a.w.) saw her, he said, "These are the kinds of clothes which have been prohibited in *Sūrah Nūr* (because they show off your beauty)." He then asked Asma to change into something different. (*Baihaqī*, vol. 7, p. 86)

In another Hadīth, Dahyah Kalabī (r.a.) narrated: Once the Prophet (s.a.w.) was presented with some material from Egypt called *Qibtiyah.* He gave me a piece of it and said, "Make a shirt for you from this and give the rest to your wife to make her scarf, but ask her to put a lining underneath so that her body cannot be seen through it." (*Abū Dāwūd*, vol. 2, p. 212)

Once 'Āishah's (r.a.) cousin, Hafsah Bint Abdul Rahmān, came to visit her. She was wearing a scarf made of thin material. 'Āishah (r.a.) took it and ripped it up and gave her one of her own scarves made of thicker material. (*Mu'attā Imām Mālik*)

On another occasion, some women from the tribe of *Banū Tamīm* came to visit 'Āishah (r.a.). They were wearing dresses made of very thin material. When 'Āishah (r.a.) saw them, she said, "If you are Mu'min, this is not a type of dress suitable for Mu'min women. But, if you are not Mu'min, then do as you please." (*Qurtubī*, vol. 14, p. 244)

Abū Hurairah (r.a.) narrated that the Prophet (s.a.w.) once said, "Two kinds of folks would be in the worst situation in Hell. First, those officials who would carry with them whips looking like the tails of cows, and they would use them for whipping people. Second, those women who would be naked despite wearing clothes (due to wearing see-through and tight clothes); they would attract strangers (men) towards them and will themselves be attracted to them. Their heads will be hanging on a side like the humps of fast camels. They will neither enter Paradise nor would even smell the fragrance of it despite the fact that the fragrance of Paradise will reach far distances." (*Muslim*)

In another Hadīth, Ibn 'Umar (r.a.) narrated that the Prophet (s.a.w.) said, "In the last days of my *Ummah*, there will be women who would be naked despite wearing clothes; their heads (due to their hair styles) would look like the humps of slim fast camels. If you see them, curse them, because they will be deprived of the Mercy of Allah. If there were to be another *Ummah* after you, these women of yours will be their servants in the same way as the women of the previous *Ummah* serve you." (*Musnad Ahmad*)

TOUCHING *GHAIR-MAHRAM* WOMEN

It is not permissible to look at *Ghair-Mahram* women due to the danger of creating *Fitnah*. Similarly, it is also not permissible to touch a *Ghair-Mahram* woman, because there the danger of creating *Fitnah* is even greater.

24.

عن معقل بن يسار رضي الله عنه عن رسول الله صلي الله عليه وسلم قال لان يطعن في رأس احدكم بمخيط من حديد خير له من ان يمس إمرأة لا تحل له

(طبراني، بيهقي)

Ma'qal Bin Yasār (r.a.) narrated that the Prophet (s.a.w.) said, "It is better that a steel nail is driven into your head than for you to touch a woman who is not permissible for you." (*Tabrānī, Baihaqī*)

There is another narration in which the Prophet (s.a.w.) has been reported to have said, "A man who touches a woman who is not legitimate for him in any way, will have a burning coal placed on his palm on the Day of Judgement." (*Mabsūt*, vol. 10, p. 152)

In another Hadīth, the Prophet (s.a.w.) has said, "Protect yourself from visiting a *Ghair-Mahram* woman in privacy. I swear by the One who has my life in His Hand, when a man visits a (*Ghair-Mahram*) woman in privacy, Shaitān is always between them. It is better for any one of you to collide with a pig covered completely in mud than to rub your shoulder against the shoulder of a woman who is not permissible for you." (*Tabrānī*)

DESCRIBING OTHER WOMEN'S ATTRIBUTES TO HUSBAND

Describing another woman's virtues, especially her physical attributes, may cause undesirable thoughts and sometimes may lead to a secret attraction and desire for the other woman. Therefore, the *Sharī'ah* has prohibited women to describe other women's attributes to their husbands.

25.

عن ابن مسعود رضي الله عنه قال قال رسول الله صلي الله عليه وسلم لا تباشرالمرأة المرأة حتي تصفها لزوجها كانه ينظر اليها (بخاري، ابوداؤد)

'Abdullah Ibn Mas'ūd (r.a.) narrated that the Prophet (s.a.w.) said, "A woman should not look at or touch another woman so that she may describe this woman to her husband in such a way as if he was actually looking at her." (*Bukhārī, Abū Dāwūd*)

Mullā Alī Qārī wrote in the interpretation of the above Hadīth: The scholars of Islam have also deduced from this Hadīth that describing the attributes of something is just like seeing it. Thus, when a woman begins to describe another woman to her husband, it is as if she is helping him to visualize that woman, which may mentally arouse him and may even lead him into the forbidden zone.

This tells us that even thinking about and imagining the looks of a *Ghair-Mahram* woman is forbidden in *Sharī'ah.* In one Hadīth, the Prophet (s.a.w.) has said, "A man, who thinks about the body of a woman under her clothes until he can visualize her shape, will not even smell the fragrance of Paradise." (*Albahr-ul Rā'iq*, vol. 8, p. 218)

WEARING NOISY ORNAMENTS

Just as looking at women's bodies is sexually exciting for men, listening to their voice and the sound of their trinkets may also arouse men. We have previously discussed, in the interpretation of some Qur'ānic Verses, how a woman should speak to strange men.

26.

عن بنانة رضي الله عنها مولاة عبدالرحمن بن حيان
الأنصاري كانت عند عائشه اذ دخلت عليها بجارية و
عليها جلاجل يصوتن فقالت لا تدخلنها علي إلا تقطعتن
جلاجلها سمعت رسول الله صلي الله عليه وسلم يقول لا
تدخل الملائكة بيتا فيه جرس (ابوداؤد، مشكوة)

Banānah (r.a.) reported: I was with 'Āishah (r.a.) when a woman with a young girl came to visit her. That girl was wearing a tinkling anklet. 'Āishah (r.a.) asked the woman, "Do not bring the girl inside the house until she removes the anklet. I have heard from the Prophet (s.a.w.) that angels do not enter the house where bells ring." (*Abū Dāwūd*, *Mishkāt*)

Abū Amāmah (r.a.) reported that the Prophet (s.a.w.) said, "Allah dislikes the sound of a tinkling anklet as much as singing; and Allah will punish the singer and the one who listens to the music similarly; and only the woman, who is far from the Mercy of Allah, will wear the tinkling anklets." (*Firdaus Al-Dailmī*)

In chapter 1, under the Qur'ānic Verses, it has already been said that while walking, women should not strike their feet on the ground so hard that *Ghair-Mahram* men may listen to the noise of their ornaments. In the above Hadīth, even the tinkling ornaments were declared undesirable and prohibited. Imagine, when it is forbidden to even have the sound of ornaments reach the *Ghair-Mahram* men, how much more undesirable it would be for a woman to either show herself or talk with *Ghair-Mahram* men.

ENTERING SOMEBODY'S HOUSE WITH PERMISSION

People live very casually in their homes. Often, they are dressed casually as well since there are no strangers around. This is why the *Sharī'ah* has commanded that no one should enter anybody's house without permission.

27.

عن عطاء بن يسار رضي الله عنه ان رسول الله صلى الله عليه وسلم ساله رجل فقال يارسول الله استاذن علي امي فقال نعم فقال الرجل اني معها في البيت فقال رسول الله صلي الله عليه وسلم استاذن عليها فقال الرجل اني خادمها فقال رسول الله صلي الله عليه وسلم استاذن عليها اتحب ان تراها عريانه قال لا قال استاذن عليها (موطا امام مالك، ص٧٢٦)

'Atā Bin Yasār narrated that once somebody asked the Prophet (s.a.w.), "O Prophet of Allah! Do I need to take permission even from my mother before entering her house?" He replied, "Yes." The man asked, "O Prophet of Allah! I live alone with her in the house." Even then he replied, "Ask for her permission." The man said, "But, I serve her." The Prophet (s.a.w.) replied, "Ask your mother for permission before entering the house. Do you wish to see her in nude?" The man replied, "No." He said, "Then ask for her permission." (*Mu'attā Imām Mālik*, p. 726)

If it was commanded to take permission from one's own mother before entering the house, it is even more important to seek the permission of others before entering their houses.

Actually, seeking permission before entering somebody's house is imperative in maintaining *Hijāb*. If anyone can march into any house without announcement, how can *Hijāb* be maintained within the house? This is why there are very clear Commands in the Ahādīth in this regard.

'Abdullah Bin Busar (r.a.) narrated that the Prophet (s.a.w.) said, "When a person goes to visit someone, he should not stand right in front of the door, but to the right or left of it." (*Abū Dāwūd*)

Obviously, if one stands right in front of the door, he/she can see inside the house when the door is opened, which is prohibited.

In another Hadīth, the Prophet (s.a.w.) said, "One who peeked inside the house before having granted the permission to come in, did not truly ask for permission." (*Abū Dāwūd*)

Abū Hurairah (r.a.) reported that the Prophet (s.a.w.) said, "You would have no blame if somebody peeks inside your house without permission and you hit him with a stone and it damages his eye." (*Bukhārī, Muslim*)

Anas (r.a.) reported that once a bedouin came to visit the Prophet (s.a.w.) and peeked into his house from a hole in the door. When the Prophet (s.a.w.) saw him, he picked up an iron rod or a wood stick and moved it towards the hole to poke it in his eye. When the bedouin saw this, he moved back. He told him, "If you had not moved back, I would have damaged your eye." (*Nasāī*)

Sahal Bin Sa'ad (r.a.) narrated that once the Prophet (s.a.w.) was in his house combing his hair when someone came and peeked through the hole in the door. When the Prophet (s.a.w.) opened the door and noticed him peeking, he told him, "If I had known before that you were peeking, I would have struck your eye with the spear." The requirement to ask for permission before entering someone's home is meant to prevent people from freely looking in. (*Bukhārī, Muslim*)

CHAPTER THREE

COMMANDMENTS OF *HIJĀB*

THE ISLAMIC SYSTEM FOR THE PREVENTION OF OBSCENITIES

After having discussed the Verses of the Holy Qur'ān and Ahādīth, it now seems appropriate to present a bird's eye view of all the Commandments Islam has provided about *Hijāb*, and the system it advocates for the prevention of indecencies and obscenities in a society.

Obscenities, immorality, adultery and all that leads to it are among those dangerous evils which often destroy not only the persons involved in them, but also families, communities and, at times, great nations. Behind many murders and other heinous crimes today, a thorough investigation often reveals a web of lust and women. This is why no nation, no religion and no region of this world has ever disagreed with the evils of obscenities and immorality.

In the last era of this world, western societies have broken their own religious values and traditions in promoting sexual freedom. They have thrown their societies and civilizations in a sexual anarchy where there is an open invitation for all to engage in indecency and immorality. However, they could not ignore the criminal consequences of such freedom, and had to declare prostitution, rape, and public sex as crimes. This is like somebody who lights and fuels a fire in a forest and then begins to worry about controlling the flames. Or, like someone who puts his pot on a burning fire and then tries to stop it from boiling over.

Contrarily, Islam not only declares such harmful and criminal activities as severely punishable, but it also regulates and prohibits any other related activities which may lead to these heinous crimes. For example, since the purpose was to safeguard human societies from rape, adultery, and immorality, the regulations commenced from asking people to lower their gaze and to stop free and unchecked mixing of sexes. Then it asked women to stay in their homes and to cover themselves completely when they emerge, to walk on the sides of street, and not to wear perfumes or noisy trinkets. And, for those who disregard all these limits, it prescribed such severe punishments that it may serve as a lesson and deterrent for the rest of the society.

In order to justify their obscenities, the westerners and their followers have put forward a number of arguments about how harmful it would be, psychologically, socially and economically, to keep women in *Hijāb*. Many contemporary scholars have countered these arguments in detail. For our purpose here, it is sufficient to understand that even crimes, such as stealing, robbing, and deceiving have their pay-offs, but when you look at the destructive consequences of such activities, you don't dare call them profitable. Even if there were some social and economical gains in bringing women out of *Hijāb*, no intelligent person could call it beneficial if it also resulted in destroying the moral fibre of a whole society and destruction of an entire nation with thousands of crimes and widespread immorality.

CUTTING OFF THE MEANS - THE GOLDEN PRINCIPLE OF PREVENTING CRIMES

As the beliefs about Oneness of Allah, Prophets, and Day of Judgement have been common and consistent in the Divine Law brought by all the Prophets; similarly, all religious laws have consistently forbidden all wrongful and indecent things. The previous religions did not absolutely forbid the means until they were used in committing a crime. However, since the *Sharī'ah* brought by the Prophet (s.a.w.) was to remain in effect till the Day of Judgement, Allah protected it by forbidding all such means which, left to their potentialities, may lead to the wrongful, indecent and criminal activities. For example, along with drinking, making wine, selling it and even serving it were forbidden. Similarly along with usuary (interest), all activities related to it were forbidden as well. Thus, the jurists declared all such profits unlawful which were received through wrongful deals. Idol-worship and associating deities with Allah are considered as major and unpardonable sins in Islam. Therefore, all the causes and means of these sins are strictly regulated as well. For example, the polytheists used to worship the sun at the time of its rising, setting and at mid day; therefore, it was forbidden for Muslims to say their prayers during those times to avoid similarity with the polytheists. And, since making of idols and pictures were means of idol-worships, these trades were prohibited as well.

In the same way, when the *Sharī'ah* prohibited illegitimate sex and adultery, it also prohibited all the means leading to it. For example, it is very clear from Ahādīth that to look at a *Ghair-Mahram* member of the opposite sex with lust was declared as the adultery of eyes, and to hear them talk, and to touch them, and to roam around looking for them were all declared as adultery of ears, hands and feet respectively.

However, there is a long range of causes and means. If all of these are to be prohibited, life will become very difficult and movements will be quite restricted, which is against the nature of this *Sharī'ah*. The Holy Qur'ān openly declares: مَا جَعَلَ عَلَيْكُمْ فِي الدِّيْنِ مِنْ حَرَجٍ "And (Allah) has imposed no undue restriction on you in this Dīn." (*Sūrah Hajj*, v. 78) This is why the restrictions on the causes and means of forbidden things have been wisely placed in this way:

1. Those activities which are so closely related to a sin that they would most likely lead a person to it have been forbidden as well.

2. Those activities which are distantly related to a sin and may not necessarily lead to it have been declared as undesirable (*Makrūh*).

3. And, activities which bear no direct relation with a sin and rarely lead a person to it have been included in permissible activities (*Mubahāt*).

The example of #1 above is liquor trade which is so closely related to drinking that it has been forbidden as well. Similarly, touching a *Ghair-Mahram* woman with lust is not quite adultery, but because it may very likely lead to it, it has been forbidden too.

The example of #2 above is selling grapes to a wine-maker, who admits to buying them to make wine. Although it is not forbidden to sell grapes, but in this case it will be considered undesirable (*Makrūh*) and not permissible. In the same way, to rent a building for the purpose of running a bank or a theatre or any other forbidden activities would be undesirable as well.

The example of #3 above is selling grapes to people at large. Although, it is possible that some may buy them for making wine, but as long as the seller did not have any foreknowledge of it, his trade is quite permissible (*Mubāh*).

It is also important to remember that if the *Sharī'ah* has declared any mean or cause of a sin as forbidden, it remains forbidden whether it does or does not lead to committing that sin under a specific situation. Disputing such a ruling is also forbidden.

The *Hijāb* for women is also based on the same principle of cutting-off-the-means, as not observing it is very likely to lead to other sins. The above three principles will apply here as well. For example, uncovering the body in front of a *Ghair-Mahram*, due to its closeness to other sins, is forbidden. Although it may not lead some people to further sins, it is absolutely forbidden with the exception of when it is required for the purpose of medical treatment, etc. It is not influenced by circumstances or time either. It was forbidden in the early days of Islam and it continues to be forbidden now.

An example of the second and the third principle in this regard is for women to emerge from their houses covered with *Burqa'* or wrapped in a long cover-all. If it is likely to lead to *Fitnah*, it will be undesirable and not permissible. But if these potentials are not present, it is permissible. Thus, the Commandment about it may change depending upon the circumstances. In the times of the Prophet (s.a.w.), it was not likely to cause *Fitnah* for women to emerge from their homes. Therefore, he had given them permission to come to the Masjid (mosque) wearing a *Burqa'* or a cover-all. Although he persuaded them to offer their *Salāt* in their homes as it was more rewarding for them to do so, he did not stop them from coming to the Masjid (mosque) since there was no likelihood of *Fitnah* at that time. After the Prophet (s.a.w.) passed away, when the Companions noticed that it was no longer safe for women to come to the Masjid (mosque), even if they came wearing a *Burqa'*, they unanimously decided to ask them not to come to the Masjid (mosque) for Jama'ah. 'Āishah (r.a.) once said that if the Prophet (s.a.w.) would have seen the present circumstances, he would have also stopped women from going to the Masjid (mosque). This shows that the decision of the Companions was not any different than what the Prophet (s.a.w.) might have done. Since those conditions were no longer present under which the Prophet (s.a.w.) had permitted it, the decision had to be changed in this regard as well.

THE HISTORY OF THE COMMANDMENTS OF *HIJĀB*

In the history of mankind, from Adam (a.s.) to Prophet Muhammad (s.a.w.), free and unchecked mixing of men and women was never considered right. Not only in the *Sharī'ah* of these Prophets, but even in noble families of the world, such free mixing has not been tolerated.

In the journey of Mūsa (a.s.) to *Madyan*, we read that the women were waiting away from the well to get water for their sheep, because they did not think it right to go amongst the crowd of men to get water.

On the occasion of the wedding of Zainab Bin Jahsh (r.a.), the first Verse of *Hijāb* was revealed. Even before this Verse was revealed, she had been reported, in a narration in Tirmizī, to be sitting in her house facing the wall "و هي موليكه وجهها الي الحائط."

One can see that the free mixing of men and women and unchecked socializing between them was not a tradition among the noble families even before the first Verse of *Hijāb* was revealed. The Ancient Age of *Jāhilīyah* and women's moving about enticingly has been discussed in Qur'ān. But only the slave girls and street women were involved in such behaviour. The noble Arab families considered such behaviour indecent and improper. The entire history of the Arabs confirms this.

In India, the Hindus, Buddhists and other idol-worshippers also did not accept unchecked mixing of men and women. It was the Western societies which, when they left their own traditional values, brought their women out to work, to go to school, clubs and parties and to freely mix with men in all aspects of their lives.

As Allah created women physically different than men; similarly, He blessed them with a natural sense of honour and decency which they preserve by remaining separate from men and by covering themselves. This natural tendency to guard their honour and modesty has been there in women since the beginning of the human race. Thus *Hijāb* was being observed in some form in the early days of Islam as well.

The particular requirements of *Hijāb* to stay home and to emerge when necessary, covering the entire body, were placed in the fifth year of Hijrah to Madīnah. The scholars of Islam have a consensus that the first Verse about *Hijāb* - لا تَدْخُلُوا بُيُوْتَ النَّبِيِّ - "Enter not the Prophet's houses...." (*Sūrah Ahzāb*, v. 53), was revealed on the occasion of Zainab's (r.a.) wedding to the Prophet (s.a.w.) which occurred in the fifth year of Hijrah. Hāfiz Ibn Hajar in *Asābah* and Ibn Abdul Bur in *Al-Iste'āb* have reported that the wedding took place in either third or fifth year of Hijrah. However, Ibn Kathīr and Ibn Sa'd have reported that it took place in fifth year of Hijrah. 'Āishah's (r.a.) narrations also seem to confirm this date. *Wallāhu A'lam.*

In the above Verse, women were directed to stay behind *Hijāb* and men were commanded to ask for things they might need from them from behind a curtain. Thus, it was stressed that women should normally remain separated from men, and that, if need be, men should talk to them from behind a curtain.

As it was mentioned previously, all scholars have agreed that لا تَدْخُلُوا بُيُوْتَ النَّبِيِّ إِلاَّ أَنْ يُؤْذَنَ لَكُمْ was the first Verse revealed related to *Hijāb*. The three Verses of *Sūrah Nūr* and the beginning Verse of *Sūrah Ahzāb* - وَ قَرْنَ فِي بُيُوْتِكُنَّ, in which the Wives of the Prophet (s.a.w.) were asked to remain in their homes, were revealed later even though these Verses appear earlier in the order of the Holy Qur'ān. This is clarified in the first Verse of *Sūrah Ahzāb* when Allah gave the Consorts of the Prophet (s.a.w.) the choice of seeking divorce from him if they preferred the bounties of this world, or to stay with him if they can be content to live with him in poverty. In the interpretation of this Verse, it is noted that Zainab Bint Jahsh (r.a.) was also included in this address. Therefore, we know that Zainab (r.a.) was already married to the Prophet (s.a.w.) at that time, and that this Verse was revealed later. Similarly, the three Verses of *Sūrah Nūr*, containing further clarification of the Commandment of *Hijāb*, also appear earlier on in the order of the Holy Qur'ān, but these were also revealed later during the Battle of *Bani Al-Mustalik* and the event of *Ifk* both of which took place in the 6th year of Hijrah. The Commandment of *Hijāb* was in effect since the marriage of Zainab (r.a.) and the Revelation of the Verse of *Hijāb*.

THE DIFFERENCE BETWEEN *HIJĀB* AND *SATR*

It is required in *Sharī'ah* for men and women to cover those parts of the body which are known as *'Aurah* in Arabic or *Satr* in Persian and Urdu. After *Īmān*, the first obligation on a Muslim is to cover these parts of his/her body. This has been an obligation since the beginning of man and in the *Sharī'ah* of all the Prophets. Even before the man was sent to this earth, when Allah took away the dress of Paradise from Adam (a.s.) and Hawwa (a.s.) as a result of disobeying Allah's Command not to taste the fruit of the forbidden tree, both of them covered their *Satr* with leaves. This is the meaning of the Verse طَفِقَا يَخۡصِفَانِ عَلَيۡهِمَا مِن وَرَقِ ٱلۡجَنَّةِ. Thus, it even seems to be a part of human nature and instinct to cover the private parts of his/her body.

In all the *Sharī'ah*, from Adam (a.s.) to the last of the Prophets, Muhammad Mustafā (s.a.w.), it has been obligatory to cover the *Satr*. There might have been minor differences in the limits and determination of the parts that must be covered, but it is universally accepted that covering certain parts of the body has been a part of the *Sharī'ah* of all the Prophets. Each man and woman is obliged to follow this Command regardless of whether somebody is watching him or not. Thus, if a person is offering his/her prayers in the nude on a dark night where there is no one to watch him, his/her prayer is unanimously unacceptable by the Islamic jurists. Similarly, if one is offering his/her prayer in a place where nobody is watching him and if his/her *Satr* becomes exposed during the prayer, the prayers become invalid.

There is no disagreement about covering the *Satr* in front of others, but, even when there is nobody to watch, it is not permissible to be naked without any physical or *Shar'ī* necessity. (*Al-bahr, Sharah Al-Muniyah*)

This is the Commandment about *Satr* which has been in effect in the *Sharī'ah* of all the Prophets since the beginning, and has been equally applicable to both men and women. So, it is not permissible to be naked in front of others or while one is alone unless it is out of necessity.

Now, about women observing *Hijāb* in front of *Ghair-Mahram* men, at least one thing has always been true among the Prophets, pious people, and noblemen, that they did not approve of unchecked mixing of men and women. There is the story of Shuaib's (a.s.) two daughters in the Holy Qur'ān where they went to the well to get water for their sheep. When they saw a crowd of men at the well, they stood on a side waiting. When Mūsa (a.s.) passed by them, he asked them the reason for standing on the side. They told him two things: 1. "There is a crowd of men by the water. We are waiting for them to leave before we get water for our sheep," and 2) "Our father is very old," meaning that it was not the work of women to go out and get the water for the sheep, but since there was nobody else around to do this work, they had to take this responsibility.

The above story in the Holy Qur'ān clearly shows that even in those days it was not preferable in their *Sharī'ah* for men and women to be together unchecked, and that women were not expected to take responsibilities which would bring them together with men. It seems that women were not commanded to observe *Hijāb* in those days which was also the case in the early days of Islam. It was in the 3rd or 5th year of Hijrah that women were commanded to observe *Hijāb* in front of *Ghair-Mahram* men.

It should be clear by now that the *Satr* and *Hijāb* for women are two different things. Observation of *Satr* has always been obligatory, whereas *Hijāb* for women was made obligatory in the 5th year of Hijrah. *Satr* is obligatory on both men and women while *Hijāb* is only required of women. *Satr* is obligatory whether one is alone or with others, while *Hijāb* is obligatory only in the presence of *Ghair-Mahram* men. A lack of distinction between these two concepts often leads to doubts, misunderstanding and misinterpretation of the Commandments of the Holy Qur'ān. For example, the face and the palms of a woman are clearly exempted from the *Satr*. Therefore, *Salāt* is permissible for a woman without covering her face and palms. The jurists have also exempted the feet of a woman from the *Satr* as well, based on the same principle.

THE CATEGORIES OF *SHARA'Ī HIJĀB* AND THEIR COMMANDMENTS

From the seven Verses of the Holy Qur'ān and numerous Ahādīth about the *Hijāb*, the primary objective seems to be to conceal women, their activities and movements from men. This is only possible by having them stay within the four walls of their homes and behind curtains. The other methods of observing *Hijāb* may be used, as required, dependent upon the needs and circumstances.

Thus the first category of *Hijāb*, which is the principal purpose of *Sharī'ah*, is for women to remain in their homes. But, Islamic *Sharī'ah* is a comprehensive and complete system of life which makes concession for all human needs. Inevitably, women will need to come out of their homes at times, which is provided for in the second category of *Hijāb*. On the basis of the Holy Qur'ān and *Sunnah*, this seems to be to cover themselves from head to toe with a *Burqa'* or cloak with a veil or holes in front of their eyes. The details of these two categories of *Hijāb* are as follows:

FIRST CATEGORY OF *HIJĀB* - REMAINING IN HOME

According to the Holy Qur'ān and *Sunnah*, this is the main objective and the principle category of *Hijāb*. The Verse in *Sūrah Ahzāb*, وَ إِذا سَأَلْتُمُوْهُنَّ مَتَاعًا فَاسْئَلُوْهُنَّ مِنْ وَّرَاءِ حِجَاب "And when you ask (his Wives) for anything you want, ask them from behind a screen...." (*Sūrah Ahzāb*, v. 53), is a clear evidence of this. Even a clearer evidence is in the earlier Verse of *Sūrah Ahzāb*: وَ قَرْنَ فِي بُيُوْتِكُنَّ "And stay quietly in your house..." (*Sūrah Ahzāb*, v. 33). The interpretation of this Verse becomes even more clear by the way the Prophet (s.a.w.) implemented it.

It has been said before that the first Verse of *Hijāb* was revealed at the time of Zainab's (r.a.) wedding to the Prophet (s.a.w.). In the Hadīth about the time of Revelation of this Verse, Anas (r.a.) reported: "I know the occasion of the Revelation of this Verse better than anybody else because I was with the Prophet (s.a.w.). When this Verse was revealed, the Prophet (s.a.w.) drew a curtain in his tent between Zainab (r.a.) and the men present in the tent." He did not ask Zainab (r.a.) to cover herself with a *Burqa'* or a sheet of cloth. The Hadīth of 'Umar (r.a.) in this regard, which has been mentioned before, also points to the same thing that the Prophet's Wives should be staying inside their homes away from the sights of men, as is evident from these words: "All kinds of good and bad people come to visit you."

In *Bukhārī*, 'Āishah (r.a.) narrated about the Battle of *Mūtah*: "The Prophet (s.a.w.) was in Masjid-Al-Nabawī when he received the news that Zaid Bin Hārithah (r.a.), Ja'far (r.a.) and 'Abdullah Bin Rawāhah (r.a.) were martyred. The signs of deep sorrow and sadness were evident from his face. I was watching the whole event from a rift in the door."

It is clear that 'Āishah (r.a.) did not come out in a *Burqa'* to participate with men even at such a sad loss. Instead, she observed the whole thing from a rift in the door of her house.

In *Bukhārī*, Book of *Battles*, Chapter of *'Umrat-ul Qada'*, it is mentioned that 'Urwah Bin Zubair (r.a.), the cousin of 'Āishah (r.a.), and 'Abdullah Bin 'Umar were sitting outside the house of 'Āishah (r.a.) talking about the occasions of *'Umrah* of the Prophet (s.a.w.). Ibn 'Umar narrated: "As we talked, we heard 'Āishah (r.a.) brushing her teeth and cleaning her throat." This also suggests that, after the Revelation of the Verse of *Hijāb*, it had become a practice of the Wives of the Prophet (s.a.w.) to observe *Hijāb* by staying in their homes.

Similarly, in *Bukhārī*, there is a Hadīth about the battle of *Tā'if* that the Prophet (s.a.w.) rinsed his mouth in a pot and gave the water to Abū Mūsa (r.a.) and Bilāl (r.a.) to drink and to rub it on their faces. *Ummul Mu'minīn* Ummi Salamah (r.a.) was watching this from behind a curtain; she asked the two Companions to leave some of that water for her as well.

This Hadīth is also an evidence that the Wives of the Prophet (s.a.w.) used to stay in their homes and behind curtains after the Verse of *Hijāb* was revealed.[15]

---

[15] It is also noteworthy from this Hadīth that the Wives of the Prophet (s.a.w.) were as eager to receive the leftover food and water of the Prophet (s.a.w.) as the rest of the Muslims. This was a special characteristic of the Holy Prophet; otherwise, the frank and close

In *Bukhārī*, *Book of Adab*, Anas (r.a.) narrated that he and Abū Talhah were once going somewhere with the Prophet (s.a.w.). The Prophet was riding a camel and behind him was *Ummul Mu'minīn* Safiyah (r.a.). On the way, his camel suddenly slipped and both of them fell. Abū Talha jumped from his camel and said, "O Allah's Apostle! May I be sacrificed for you; are you hurt?" The Prophet said, "No, take care of the lady." So, Abū Talhah covered his face with a garment and went to Safiyah and covered her with it, and then he set right the condition of their camel so that both of them rode...

In the above incident, the precautions of the Companions to observe *Hijāb* with the Wives of the Prophet (s.a.w.), even in the event of an accident, signifies the importance of it.

In *Tirmizī* there is a Hadīth narrated by 'Abdullah Bin Mas'ūd that the Prophet (s.a.w.) said: اذا خرجت المرأة استشرفها الشيطن "When a woman emerges from her home, Shaitān waits for an opportunity (i.e., he uses her to spread mischief among Muslims)."

Ibn Khuzaimah and Ibn Habbān, in their narration of the above Hadīth, have added these words: اقرب ما تكون من وجه ربها و هي في قعر بيتها "A woman is closest to her Creator when she is concealed in her home."

This Hadīth also confirms that women should remain in their homes unless it was necessary for them to emerge.

In another Hadīth, the Prophet (s.a.w.) has said: ليس للنساء نصيب في الخروج إلا مضطرة "Women should not come out of their homes except under a dire necessity." (*Tabrānī*, *Kanaz-ul Ummāl*, vol. 8. p. 263)

(cont. from p. 93) relationship between a man and his wife does not naturally permit to observe such reverence and respect of the spouse.

Ali (r.a.) narrated: Once I was in the presence of the Prophet (s.a.w.); he asked the Companions, اي شئ خير للنساء "What is better for women?" Nobody responded. The Companions remained silent. When I went home and asked Fātimah the same question. She replied, لا يرين الرجال و لا يرونهن "It is better for women that they don't look at men, nor be looked at by men." I repeated her answer to the Prophet (s.a.w.). He said, صدقت انها بضعته مني "She responded correctly; indeed she is a part of me."

In the incident of *Ifk*, the reason why 'Āishah Siddīqah (r.a.) was left in the jungle, was the fact that the *Hijāb* of the Wives of the Prophet was not limited to *Burqa'* or a wrapped around sheet, but even while travelling, they remained in their *Haudaj*. This *Haudaj* was lifted and placed upon a camel and brought down (without being looked inside). The *Haudaj* was like a home for travelling ladies. In this incident, when the caravan was ready to move, the servants lifted the *Haudaj* and mounted it on the back of the camel assuming that 'Āishah (r.a.) was inside, but she was not in it. She had gone away from the caravan out of necessity. Thus, the caravan left and she was left alone in the jungle.

This incident also confirms that the Prophet (s.a.w.) and his Wives interpreted the *Shara'ī* requirement of *Hijāb* for women to stay in their homes and inside the *Haudaj* during the travel, so that they are not in front of men. If they were so vigilant about observing *Hijāb* even when they were travelling, how much more would they have cared for it while at home?

SECOND CATEGORY OF *HIJĀB* - BY *BURQA'*

When a woman has to come out of her home under necessity, she is required to emerge in *Burqa'* or wrapped in a long sheet of cloth from head to toe, which does not reveal any part of her body. This is confirmed by the following Verse of

Sūrah Ahzāb: يٰايها النبي قل لازواجك وبنٰتك ونساء المؤمنين يدنين عليهن من جلابيبهن "O Prophet! Tell your Wives and daughters and the believing women that they should cast their *Jalābīb* (outer garments) over their persons..." (*Sūrah Ahzāb*, v. 59)

As has been mentioned previously, *Jalbāb* means a cloak or a long sheet of cloth which covers a person from head to toe.

Iḥn Jarīr has narrated from 'Abdullah Bin 'Abbās (r.a.) that this *Jalbāb* should be worn in a way so that it covers a woman from head to toe including her face, leaving an opening around one eye to see the road. The full interpretation of this Verse has been given in chapter 1. The intent here is to show that a woman is required to observe this second category of *Hijāb* when she comes out of her home under necessity.

Whereas it is permissible for women to observe this category of *Hijāb* under necessity, they may do so with certain other restrictions which are evident from Sahīh Ahādīth. Those are that they should not use perfumes, should not wear noisy trinkets, should walk on the sides of street and not enter in the crowds of men.

It is reported in a Hadīth that once Bilāl (r.a.) or Anas (r.a.) went to bring Hadhrat Fātimah's baby to the Prophet (s.a.w.). Fātimah (r.a.) gave him the baby from behind a curtain despite the fact that both these men were very close servants of the family and often visited the family.

After the Revelation of the Verse of *Hijāb*, curtains were hung in the houses of the Prophet (s.a.w.) as well as other Muslim homes. (*Darsi Qur'ān*, vol. 7, p. 631)

In summary, all four Imāms have agreed that it is not permissible for a woman to uncover her face in front of a *Ghair-Mahram*. Three of the four Imāms have called it absolutely forbidden, whereas Imām Abū Hanīfah and his followers have called it forbidden due to the possibility of *Fitnah*. Included among the *Ghair-Mahram* men are, the husband's brother, the sister's husband, the husband of husband's sister, and the sons of uncles and aunts. Often these men are mistakenly considered *Mahārim* despite the fact that the Prophet (s.a.w.) have declared all of them as *Ghair-Mahram*, as has been mentioned previously under chapter two on Ahādīth.

In uncovering the face in front of *Ghair-Mahram* men, the possibility of *Fitnah* is so evident that one does not need to elaborate upon it. No household is free from such incidents of *Fitnah*, but since people generally tend to hide such incidents, they don't become known. Even then, every now and then such incidents are published in the news papers. In order to give you some examples, I would mention some such incidents.

In one of his published speeches, Muftī Rashīd Ahmad Karāchwī mentioned:

"Some people are under the misconception that they don't have any danger from not observing *Hijāb* in their homes. They say, 'Masha-Allah, our wives, daughters, sisters and daughters-in-law are very pious. Their eyes are not cast on any thing bad, so how can they have any bad intentions in their hearts. Our brothers and other relatives, like the sons of uncles and aunts, are all from noble families. We cannot even imagine such bad things in our household'.

People are often as careless in this matter as it is important. Even very learned scholars are careless in this regard. People ignore to follow the clear Commandment of the Holy Qur'ān as if this Commandment (of *Hijāb*) was never revealed in the Holy Qur'ān.

I will tell you some incidents in families who thought of themselves as very pious. Like yourselves, they began to take pride in their piety and threw behind their backs the Commandment of Allah by not observing *Hijāb* in their homes. What were the results? These are not stories of past. These incidents have occurred recently here in Karachi. If it was not for maintaining the honour of their families, I would have told you their names and addresses so that you could go and ask them and verify these incidents yourself. The truth is that they dishonoured their families and themselves by breaking the Commandment of Allah about *Hijāb*. Now listen to these stories. May these penetrate your hearts."

First Incident

"There was a Haji Sahib, a very pious and virtuous man. People had such faith in his piety that they had entrusted him with their valuables, worth millions. Once some of his relatives came to me and told me of this incident. He fell in love with his sister-in-law. His wife and his in-laws all lived in the same house; and he ended up having an illegitimate relationship with his sister-in-law. What did he do? He quietly obtained a passport and visa of a foreign country, shaved off his beard, put on a suit and ran off to this foreign country with all the things that people had placed in his trust. Think about it; people say that there is no possibility of such a thing happening in their homes and that their home environment is very pious and clean. What can you say about such self deceptions and vain hopes?"

Second Incident

"This also happened in Karachi. A man, who was very religious and an enthusiastic participant in religious activities and who also had the good fortune of performing *Hajj*, ended up having an illegitimate affair with his sister-in-law simply because there was no tradition of observing *Hijāb* in his home. Their relationship continued for many years, during which the woman kept taking birth control pills, until she got married and went to her husband's house."

Third Incident

"A man, who observed his *Salāt* and Fasting regularly and his wife was also from a noble family, did not observe *Hijāb* in his home. They often visited their friends, and their friends came to their house openly. Once, one of his friends led his wife on and they ended up having a relationship. This man worked all day, the children would be in school, and the wife had fun with her husband's friend in the privacy of her own home. After some time, the husband found out about the affair. He tried his best to stop his wife without much success, and ended up divorcing her."

I mentioned the above three incidents to give you a sample. Otherwise, there are innumerable stories like these taking place every day. It is clear that the beginning of such incidents is clearly lack of *Hijāb* in homes which is always the first step. If *Hijāb* is observed vigilantly, such things can be prevented before they begin.

CHAPTER FOUR

THE ANCIENT AGE OF *JĀHILĪYAH* AND PRESENT DAY *JĀHILĪYAH*

Thousands of years ago, two ages passed to which the Holy Qur'ān has referred as the initial Ages of *Jāhilīyah*: one is the age between the coming of the Prophets Nūh and Idrīs (a.s.) and the other between the time of Īsā (a.s.) and our Prophet (s.a.w.). The women of these ages exposed their bodies and abused their freedom to leave their homes to an extent unheard of before that time. As a result they came to be regarded as objects to be exhibited and taken advantage of by all. They were no longer like precious treasures to be protected by those whom they rightfully belonged to, but had become like public charity which could be utilized by anybody at any time. They walked the streets, well-decorated with jewelry and perfumes, attracting men with their flirtatious mannerism as well as by showing off their beauty and half-clad bodies. The frequent contact of women with men other than their husbands created a situation whereby it was possible for a woman to be used by her husband and a lover at the same time. Not having any regard for their honour, respect, chastity and modesty, these women had no hesitation to please men with anything they could ever want from a woman. It was these shameless behaviours and immoral acts of those olden days which the Holy Qur'ān referred to as *Tabarruj Al-Jāhilīyah.*

Today's licentious societies, and in particular, the West's pleasure-loving but cultured communities, have gone so far in their lewdness and indecencies that they have managed to put even the past Ages of *Jāhilīyah* and their indecencies to shame. The sexy dresses, vanity and enticement of the women along with the shameless and lewd behaviour of the men in these societies, which have all been legalized and branded as modern civilization, not only resemble the first age of *Jāhilīyah* but, in its excesses, has surpassed it.

Undoubtedly women today have their legal rights and freedom. But, in reality, what do these rights translate into except the freedom to leave their homes half-dressed without being hindered to wander in parks and other public places? Dressed provocatively in a manner which draws particular attention to the most alluring parts of her body, she walks and flirts in a way which gains her the attention of men around her. In this way, a single woman gains numerous boy-friends while the married woman creates a number of rivals for her husband. Married women openly meet and have fun with their men friends without the permission or will of their husbands. In such instances, the law does not side with the husband who does not have the right to interfere in his wife's activities since she is completely free in her own rights to do as she pleases without interference. What this means, in other words, is that the modern society is obligated not to defend and safeguard the moral values of a society, but instead to ensure that it provides all the facilities which contribute to and foster immorality and moral decay.

SEVERAL EXAMPLES OF INDECENCY IN THE PRESENT DAY *JĀHILĪYAH*

The consequence of legalizing such dishonourable behaviour has been the increasing acceptance and support of indecency by society. The Salvation Army of Europe, a service organization which was established mainly to help and look after the helpless, is also involved in helping unwed mothers during their pregnancy and delivery by providing them with maternity homes. In 1928, the Calcutta based *Forward* magazine published the following excerpt from a New York magazine which reported some findings from a paper issued by this Salvation Army.

> Twenty years ago, the majority of women availing themselves of the maternity home facilities were older, mature women who were well aware of the possible consequences of their immoral behaviour. Now the situation has changed drastically. The vast majority of women who now come to these maternity homes are in fact young students and immature girls who should be worrying about their schools rather than preparing for motherhood. According to the latest statistics these young girls represent 42% of the population of these homes and their average age is only 16.

These high numbers of unwanted pregnancies are there despite the fact that numerous methods of birth control are now easily available and getting pregnant accidentally has become almost impossible. In other words, a very small number, perhaps one out of every couple of hundreds, of those who actually engage in illicit sexual activity find themselves in a maternity home.

Despite the fact that prostitution was illegal in London and not included in the rights of women, one trustworthy source, a lady, writes:

> In the three years from 1915 to 1917 over 20,000 women were arrested in London alone for prostitution. These were only the ones who were unlucky or stupid enough to get caught, for there are in fact thousands more who have practiced this trade all their lives and have managed to elude the law. (*Inqilāb*, July 1, 1928 as quoted in *T'alīmāt-i-Islam*)

John Pull writes:

> There are over 40,000 prostitutes in New York City, not counting those girls who use their homes, hotels and other public places to carry on their trade. It has been calculated that one out of every ten women in New York is involved in such a trade and that an estimated 5,540,000 men avail themselves of their services during a year. In other words 15,180 men visit such women every day, many of whom suffer from sexually transmitted diseases. (*Inqilāb*, July 1, 1928 as quoted in *T'alīmāt-i-Islam*)

The June 1935 edition of the magazine *Mahshar-i-Khayāl* stated that 30,000 women in London practiced prostitution with a legal license. Even if such women are visited by a minimum of five men a day, which is obviously a very conservative number, then 150,000 men a day and 5,475,000 a year openly commit legal adultery in the city of London alone.

In the city of Glasgow, young women announced that they would set up kissing stands to raise money for the college students of the city. Selling a kiss for six shillings each, these young women raised thousands of pounds.

There are organized young women's associations in London whose membership vow never to marry, but having love affairs and illicit sexual relationships are not against their association's constitution.

Female students at one American university were asked in a survey to list the qualities and skills which were necessary for girls to have before entering universities for the first time. Over two hundred girls responded. A summary of the results of this survey was published in the newspaper *Siyāsat*, Lahore.

> "Girls should be aware of what is masculinity and what is femininity, their characteristics and requisites. She should know how to dance, smoke, drink, and hug a member of the opposite sex. She should not indiscriminately respond to every male who appears interested in her; instead she should select her partners on the basis of her taste and interests. She should also know how to handle herself with someone who has been drinking or is coming on too strong and against her will. One girl's response was more specific. She said that girls should have some experience beforehand in hugging and kissing men so as to prevent embarrassment due to inexperience when they go to university. Thus, they will have the ability to effectively handle themselves with other male students, teachers, or staff of the university. Also she should know how to tactfully discourage physical overtures from those she does not like. (*Siyasāt*, Lahore, May 28, 1923)

George Allen Endalon writes in his book *Civilization*:

> Words of respect are uttered in praise of the qualities of chastity, modesty and honour, but everyday life is devoted to the pursuit of adultery, fornication and syphilis. (*T'alīmāt-i-Islam*, p. 105)

These same needs for sexual excitement led to the convening of international exhibitions in West. Exhibitions of what commodity? Not of commercial items, but beauty pageants to exhibit and judge women's bodies. The purpose of these beauty pageants is to select the most beautiful woman from the respresentatives of different countries of the world. The winning country and province is then praised in glowing terms. Not only are there pageants to choose the most beautiful women, but there are shows now to choose the woman with the most beautiful body parts. Only recently there was a "most beautiful thighs" pageant, to decide which of the young women competing had the most perfect thighs, in terms of colour, size, shape, etc. The winners of such shows are awarded prizes. One can easily estimate where the values of people are headed today.

The few examples and statistics presented above, which do not represent the entire West but only a few cities and only over a limited time frame (65 years ago), are sufficient to give the readers some inkling of the extent to which male and female intermingling and immodesty have lowered human beings to the level of animals. It also clearly demonstrates the extent to which people, who have denounced religion in favour of their own man-made laws and modernization, are losing the very characteristics which make them human. While sacrificing true happiness, mental peace and satisfaction, the doors of Hell are being opened to swallow the entire human race.

This is the progressive and enlightened culture to which its avid, almost fanatical converts (our "enlightened" younger generation), are inviting us. Articles and columns opposing and misrepresenting *Hijāb* as it is defined by *Sharī'ah* fill the pages of newspapers and magazines in order to ensure that Asia follows the West on the road to shamelessness and renounces *Hijāb*. Alas, we have become dumb, deaf and blind; our hearts have been shielded from the truth, and our minds have been paralyzed. We have lost the ability to grasp the real truth and enlightenment of Islam. It was because of the dangerous and morally destructive outcomes of ignoring *Hijāb* that the Islamic *Sharī'ah* educated its followers in the ways of modesty, purity, and faith. Muslims are taught, not only to eschew the shameless immodest behaviour which characterizes both the first and second Ages of *Jāhilīyah*, but also to avoid any similarity or resemblance to it.

It is for this reason that Islam presented, against *Tabarruj Al-Jāhilīyah*, a natural alternative of *Hijāb*, which fosters modesty and ensures positive outcomes. It not only protects the honour of the virtuous Muslim women, but also guarantees material success, protection of human virtues, and national integrity.

It should be kept in mind that the above examples, which were taken from the book *Shara'ī Purdah* by Qārī Mohammed Tayyab, were from sixty years ago. In the past sixty years the Western world has witnessed a manifold increase in indecency, lewdness, and corruption in their society. It is a phenomenon of which the Western people themselves are well aware, for it is they who have created the laws which legalize and protect these new 'rights' of its citizens. Countless incidents take place on a daily basis which illustrate this. One such event took place in the city of Kitchener, Canada, and was reported by the *K.W. Record* in its October 25th, 1988 edition:

> A 40 years old Canadian immigrant of Chile lived in Canada with his 34 year old Chilean wife. One day, upon returning home he found his wife in bed with another man. He went to the police to report the incident and was told that they could not take any action as her actions were not against the law. He returned home, but once there, could not bear to simply do nothing; he called the police again. Two police officers soon arrived, appraised themselves of the situation and informed him that they could not do anything. They advised him to go to sleep on the sofa in the other room and left. Unable to control his emotions any longer, the husband picked up a knife and stabbed his wife in the back. She was admitted to the hospital for her injuries and soon recovered. No charges were brought against her. Her husband, however, was

> brought to trial and, being found guilty of stabbing his wife, was sentenced to jail for a year and a half.

Incidents such as these are commonplace here and do not surprise or astonish the local residents. It is hard to find college or university girls who remain virgin till they are married. As a matter of fact Westerners are often surprised that the people of East still expect unmarried girls to remain virgin until the time of their marriage.

A SUMMARY OF THE DETAILS OF *HIJĀB* AND THE INTENTIONS OF *SHARĪ'AH*

The rules and regulations dealing with *Hijāb* as outlined by Islamic *Sharī'ah* are so all-encompassing that virtually no part of a Muslim's life has been left untouched. The religious, social, psychological, emotional, spiritual, cognitive and deeply personal practices are all affected by the injunctions of *Hijāb* for women and *Ghadd Al-Basar* (lowering of the gaze) for men. Sound Guidance has also been given related to all hidden and apparent aspects of covering the *Satr* and lowering of the gaze. As you have read previously, the Commandments for *Hijāb* came not all at once. First, the Command for separation between men and women was revealed; then came the Commandments for concealing the body, personal beauty, and ornamentation; then about the use of perfumes, walking, talking, lowering of gaze, and covering the face. Later, the codes of behaviour with the opposite sex, addressing even the personal thoughts and fantasies about them, were revealed. All of this makes it impossible to believe, even for a moment, that the *Sharī'ah* tolerates the slightest mixing and social intimacy between unrelated men and women leading to sexual excitement of the parties. On the contrary, from all the rules and limits it has imposed on women emerging from their homes, it becomes very clear that its aim is to have women understand the intent of the *Sharī'ah* and prevent themselves from leaving their homes. Why?

So that the blatant sexual misconduct and commotion of the past or present Age of *Jāhilīyah* do not find their way into their lives. And, so that women, in their ignorance and quest for what they perceived to be the greater enjoyments of the *Jāhilīyah* culture, would not renounce their modesty, good character, and upright behaviour. Thus, as many faces and models of shamelessness, immodesty and licentious behaviour were presented by the former *Jāhilīyah*; Islamic *Sharī'ah* countered them with as many defenses and preventive measures of safeguarding modesty and honour which successfully blocked these shameless immodesties and protected the Muslim women from being affected by the degeneracy of the modern age.

A COMPARISON BETWEEN THE WOMEN OF THE EAST AND THE WEST

The noble woman of the East values and protects her modesty and chastity so highly that she veils herself, both literally and figuratively, and limits herself to the four walls of her house. The internally torn woman of the West, by contrast, exhibits everything she has to offer, attracts men and is attracted to them, and leaves her home to knock about aimlessly in cinemas and cafes, malls and bazaars, parks and theatres, exhibitions and circuses. How does one compare the sinful false vanity of *Jāhilīyah* to the billowing ocean of honour and modesty of Muslim women. As a poet has said: "How do you compare a dead lantern with the light of the sun?"

The very goals of these women of different cultures are different; with one aiming to reach a spiritually elevated character, while the other striving to attain more basic, physical desires and needs. There are likewise a myriad of other differences, both basic and secondary, mental and visible, which exist between these women. How then could it be possible for Islamic *Sharīʿah*, which is determined to end all similarities with *Jāhilīyah* culture, to permit any association between the two? And how could it tolerate any resemblances to develop between their widely differing paths? Islamic *Sharīʿah* put an end to immodesty and gave the Commandment of *Hijāb* to chaste and virtuous women so that no similarities would remain between Muslim women and the women of the old and new Ages of *Jāhilīyah*.

With all this in mind, the Muslim world cannot expect to ease up on even a minor restriction of Hijāb, thinking of it as unnecessary or unimportant, and realistically expect the rest of the laws to remain inviolable. Man's most base human urgings are such that they exert a pressure on all higher human thoughts and actions until they have brought them down to their own low level. The prevailing nudity, immodesty and indecent behaviour of modern societies did not reach their current and morally reprehensible state of affairs at once. They too reached their current state gradually by permitting small indecencies which these chaotic societies, in their lack of wisdom and foresight, thought of as harmless. It was, therefore, inevitable under the natural laws of cause and effect, that once the grip of morality began to loosen, the shamelessness and indecencies reached an epidemic proportion. The extremes to which these societies have now reached are the very horrors which the initial limitations of *Hijāb* were established to prevent. It is a characteristic of human nature that once it has crossed the first limit imposed upon it, it becomes successively easier to break other, bigger rules until, finally, all limits have been crossed.

So when the fairer sex of these nations had taken the major step of abandoning the four walls of their homes in favour of the outside world, it was comparatively easy to take the next step and break the silence of their voices, which had long gone unheard. And after this, the faces behind the veils were revealed, and with them, the gaze too was now given the freedom to wander, to see and be seen. The freedom of eyes to look around freely led to the freedom of thought which rejected the very thought of *Hijāb*. Clothes were now designed to enhance and reveal a woman's body; at first necklines and arms and then legs and thighs were exposed. Thus, all the veils were removed from the private and excitable parts of human body leading ultimately to total nudity, which was precisely what the comprehensive Commandments of *Hijāb* intended to prevent. Today, there are hundreds of thousands of nudists in these European and Western countries. The newspaper *Inqilāb* writes:

> In France and Germany a new trend of complete nudity has begun. Even an association of nudists has been established in Germany which calls itself the National Association of Nudists. Its membership has already reached four hundred thousand, of which women form a vast majority. A 1929 survey revealed that its members numbered over four million (*Inqilāb*, Lahore, Dec. 30, 1929 as quoted in *T'alīmāt-i-Islam*).

The newspaper *Madīnah* in Bajnor, India, reporting on the situation in France, writes:

> The people of France, in order to practice their beliefs in naturalism, have established a naturalists' society consisting of several thousand members. They live only on fruit, vegetables, and water, and shun clothing as much as possible, choosing to wear very skimpy bathing outfits instead. The most fanatic among them, however, refuse to wear even those, calling them unnatural and unnecessary. These members have announced that they will cast off all clothing and will live in nude. The members of this club

> include men, women, children and elderly people, and their membership is increasing every day. In Germany, the number of people claiming to be naturalists numbered three million last year, and this year the membership has increased by one million more (*Madīnah,* May 9, 1929 as quoted in *T'alīmāt-i-Islam*).

Obviously, after having reached the peak of such shamelessness, open and unhesitated sexual promiscuity and fornication is not surprising at all in the Western cultures. It was this sexual promiscuity and shamelessness which Islam eradicated by imposing the various Commandments of *Hijāb.* Do the Muslims assume that by blindly following the footsteps of these shameless societies, they will not some day end up at the same peaks of immorality as their Western tutors have already reached? Nay!

وَلَنْ تَجِدَ لِسُنَّةِ اللهِ تَبْدِيلًا (الأحزاب، ٦٢)

> You will never find a change in the ways of Allah. (*Sūrah Ahzāb*, v. 62)

The truth contained in this Verse translates into the principle that whenever Muslims abandon the teachings and practices of our Prophet (s.a.w.) in favour of using their own intelligence as their guides in life, they are destined for destruction. Salvation depends solely upon obeying the laws of Allah as revealed to our Prophet (s.a.w.), while depending solely on one's own intelligence and abilities leads only to one's downfall.

The social system which the Holy Qur'ān and the *Sunnah* have given the world is one which guarantees piety and cleanliness, purity and chastity, respect and inner peace. It is only through Islam that Allah has blessed Muslims with honour and glory. Abandoning the ways which are characteristic of

Islamic society in favour of foreign cultures and ideas, fashions and norms should be repulsive to the very self-respect of Muslims. The Christians, Jews and atheists of the West are truly dangerous enemies of Muslims. They have convinced the less knowledgeable and weaker Muslims the necessity of women's emancipation, thereby engaging them in the same kinds of lewd, indecent and immoral behaviour as they follow, in order to destroy the purity and the virtues of Islamic societies and to foster all kinds of filth within them. These enemies of Islam have insidiously laid all kinds of traps within Muslim societies, to which those Muslims who have a weak attachment to the Holy Qur'ān and *Sunnah*, fall prey with ease. إنا لله و إنا إليه راجعون. The moral destruction, lewdness and licentious behaviour that the people in Europe, America and other Western countries are suffering from today, began with bringing women out in the open. Once out in the streets, the doors were open for physical and sexual exploitations, which in turn gave way to lewdness, leading to nudity and all kinds of other immoral and shameless behaviour. A virtuous English woman, sincerely disturbed by the increasingly immoral behaviour of women in her own society, wrote an article which was translated and reproduced in an Egyptian monthly magazine, *Al-Manār*. In this article she writes:

> English women, as a whole, have lost their chastity and virtue. It has become difficult to find women who have kept themselves pure and not defiled themselves by engaging in illicit behaviour. They no longer possess any semblance of modesty or shamefulness, and live their lives with such unlimited and unnatural freedom that it has left them unworthy of being called human beings. We envy the Muslim women of the East, who live lives of honesty and piety in obedience of their husbands and who do not let the stains of sin mar their purity and chastity. If they feel pride in their ways of

life, they have every right to do so. The time is coming when the Commandments of Islamic *Sharī'ah* will come to aid and protect the virtue of English women as well. (Quoted in *Ma'ārif-ul-Qur'ān*, vol. 9, by Maulānā Idrīs Kāndhalvī)

Anyway, the Holy Qur'ān and Ahādīth have elucidated the subject of *Hijāb* with such clear and convincing arguments that there no longer remains any room for doubt or suspicion in the wisdom behind it.

A MOMENT OF THOUGHT

The above discussion makes it abundantly clear how much care Allah and His beloved Prophet (s.a.w.) have taken in presenting the Commandments of *Hijāb*, and how much detail and clarification has been provided to us of each aspect of *Hijāb*, as well as how strongly have we been asked to follow these Commandments.

As Muslims we should think! To what extent do we actually follow the Holy Qur'ān in which we profess to have such faith, and how much concern and regard do we sincerely have for its Commandments? Could it be that on the Day of Judgement, as according to the following Verse in the Holy Qur'ān, our Prophet (s.a.w.) says to Allah (regarding us):

يارَبِّ إِنَّ قَوْمِي اتَّخَذُوا هٰذَا الْقُرْاٰنَ مَهْجُوْرًا (الفرقان، ٣٠)

Oh Lord! My *Ummah* forsook this Qur'ān.... (*Sūrah Furqān*, v. 30)

We believe in Allah and it is also our belief that on the Day of Judgement all of us will have to face Him, and we will be held accountable for our each and every action. How then do we expect to meet Him? Will He not say to us: "I revealed to you clearly all the etiquettes of living your lives and made clear the difference between Halal and Haram. How closely then did you follow my Commands? How much did your character, thoughts, and actions reflect the fear of accountability before me?"

On the Day of Judgement we will face our beloved Prophet (s.a.w.) as well. With the sun unbearably close over us, it will be a day of unimaginable difficulty, torment and unendurable thirst. He will lead us all to the well of *Kauthar* to drink. But have we ever thought about how shall we face him? We, who have spent our whole lives ignoring his teachings and never taking any steps to implement them in our lives; how will we honestly expect him to quench our thirst with his own blessed hands? How can we expect that he will intervene on our behalf when we will meet him bent under the burden of our sins? Have we followed his teachings in our lifestyles, our appearances, our manners of dressing, or in anything else in our lives?

The Commandments of *Hijāb* are of great importance, though it is true that they are in fact somewhat difficult to follow. But one thing is true beyond doubt, and that is that whosoever succeeds in following these Commandments will have less difficulty in obeying other Commandments of Allah. This is one of the most bitter pills to swallow in terms of obedience, but it is most beneficial in that it makes it quick and easy for a Muslim to be close to Allah.

Today, our standards of piety have become limited to reciting endless incantations and rosaries, praying extra *Salāt*, reciting the books of prayers, fasting when possible, giving alms and charity, and obeying those Commands which are convenient for us. But, we readily ignore and reject all those rules and prohibitions which interfere in any way with our lifestyle, *Nafs* and desires. We profess deep love for Allah, but do not refrain from disobeying Him, even though it is obligatory on us to refrain from all that He has declared *Harām*. The foundation of piety is built on seeking Allah's Forgiveness for all our disobedience and rebelliousness against Him. Prophet Muhammad (s.a.w.) has said:

اتق المحارم تكن اعبد الناس

> Refrain from sinning, and you will become the most pious of worshippers.

The sin of refusing to observe *Hijāb* is more severe than other sins, which is why it is critical to immediately desist from it and to sincerely resolve not to repeat it. The reasons for this are as follows:

1. It is a sin which is committed in the open for all to see. The one committing this sin, without saying a word, is openly declaring to everyone around him that she/he has no regard for Allah's Commands, and that she/he has revolted against Allah. Our Prophet (s.a.w.) has said:

كل امتي معافي إلا المجاهرين

> All of my *Ummah* is worthy of forgiveness, except for those who have openly sinned.

This is true not only for religion, but even under the laws of any government of this world, those who openly betray their governments are not forgiven. And what is the punishment for betrayal but death?

2. The sinful consequences of refusing to observe *Hijāb* are not limited only to the one committing this sin; since it encourages and spreads lewd and shameful behaviour, it ultimately affects the entire society which thus gets caught in Allah's Punishment in this world and in the Hereafter. It is

commonly observed that such a sin also paves the way for all kinds of other mischiefs, even murder.

Those women who do not observe *Hijāb* should ask themselves why are they doing so. Is it the temporary pleasures and fulfilment of desires which is keeping them from it? They should realize that life in this world is short while life in the world Hereafter is for ever. They should also realize that by not observing *Hijāb* they are embittering their lives here as well as condemning themselves to the punishment of Hellfire in the Hereafter. We are not able to bear, even for a second, the heat of a burning coal placed on the palm of our hand. And yet we never think, how will we be able to bear the severe torment and fires of Hell? If we worry that our father or husband or other relatives will not approve and will be displeased with our following Allah's Commands, then we should also think whether this will be an acceptable excuse before Allah on the Day of Judgement. Will He forgive us if we say that we did not follow His Orders because we feared displeasing our family and friends. Even though it is Allah's absolute and unalterable Law that لا طاعته المخلوق في معصيته الخالق "Obeying anyone while disobeying Allah is forbidden." That is, if someone asks us to disobey Allah, we are forbidden to obey him. We should simply reject such a demand. We should consider whether this person, whom we are attempting to pleae by disobeying Allah, will be willing to receive and bear the punishment in our place on the Day of Judgement? Allah clearly states in the Holy Qur'ān:

إِذْ تَبَرَّأَ الَّذِينَ اتُّبِعُوا مِنَ الَّذِينَ اتَّبَعُوا وَرَأَوُا الْعَذَابَ وَ
تَقَطَّعَتْ بِهِمُ الْأَسْبَابُ ۝ وَ قَالَ الَّذِينَ اتَّبَعُوا لَوْ أَنَّ لَنَا
كَرَّةً فَنَتَبَرَّأَ مِنْهُمْ كَمَا تَبَرَّءُوا مِنَّا كَذَالِكَ يُرِيهِمُ اللهُ
أَعْمَالَهُمْ حَسَرَاتٍ عَلَيْهِمْ وَمَاهُمْ بِخَارِجِينَ مِنَ النَّارِ
(البقرة، ١٦٧-١٦٦)

> Then would those who are followed clear themselves of those who follow (them); they would see the penalty and all relations between them would be cut off. And those who followed would say, "If only we had one more chance, we would clear ourselves of them as they have cleared themselves of us." Thus will Allah show them (the fruits of) their deeds as (nothing but) regrets, nor will there be a way for them out of the Fire. (*Sūrah Baqrah*, v. 166-167)

Ponder on this Verse, and it becomes clear that on the Day of Judgement, those people who disregarded the Commands of Allah and disobeyed Him to follow and please others, will be enemies unto each other and all relations between them will be severed. On that day, the young will blame their elders for not letting them obey Allah and observe *Hijāb*, while the elders will say that they had no control over them, they only asked them to disobey, but did not force them. Then, how frustrated and helpless will those feel who had disobeyed Allah to please others around them? How sorry and miserable will those feel when they realize that the people they had tried to please and on whose account they were to endure such grave punishment, were denying all responsibility for their wrong-doing and were accusing them of being guilty instead? Let alone men, even Shaitān, on the Day of Judgement, will say:

وَقَالَ الشَّيْطَٰنُ لَمَّا قُضِيَ الْأَمْرُ إِنَّ اللَّهَ وَعَدَكُمْ وَعْدَ الْحَقِّ وَوَعَدتُّكُمْ
فَأَخْلَفْتُكُمْ ۖ وَمَا كَانَ لِيَ عَلَيْكُم مِّن سُلْطَٰنٍ إِلَّا أَن دَعَوْتُكُمْ
فَاسْتَجَبْتُمْ لِي ۖ فَلَا تَلُومُونِي وَلُومُوا أَنفُسَكُم ۖ مَّا أَنَا
بِمُصْرِخِكُمْ وَمَا أَنتُم بِمُصْرِخِيَّ ۖ إِنِّي كَفَرْتُ بِمَا
أَشْرَكْتُمُونِ مِن قَبْلُ ۗ إِنَّ الظَّالِمِينَ لَهُمْ عَذَابٌ أَلِيمٌ سورة ابراهيم

> And Shaitān will say when the matter is decided, "It was Allah Who gave you a promise of truth,

> I too promised but I failed in my promise to you. I had no authority over you except to call you but you listened to me; then reproach me not, but reproach your own souls. I cannot listen to your cries nor can you listen to mine. I reject your former act of associating me with Allah. For wrongdoers there must be a Grievous Penalty." (*Sūrah Ibrāhīm*, v. 22)

So, we know that on this day no one will come to anyone else's aid, and every human being will be left alone to answer for his own deeds. Even the Shaitān will say to those who followed him, "I had no real power over you, all I could do was to tempt and preach you; you chose to follow me and committed sins of your own free will. I am disgusted with you for associating me with Allah and obeying me in His stead. You were with me in life, and you will be with me now. We will go to Hell and abide there together."

For the Sake of Allah, think! Is the goal in life to gain Allah's Pleasure, or the pleasure of a few relatives? By Allah, those who sever their worldly relations in this life for the Sake of Allah, will attain Heaven right here on earth. He, who turned away from people and cut his relations with them solely to gain Allah's Pleasure and to avoid punishment in his final and everlasting abode in the Hereafter, has attained true success. He will be rewarded with such joy and pleasure that all the joys of this world will seem insignificant and worthless by comparison. As a poet has said:

> You shouldn't care if the entire world is angry at you;
> So long as your beloved is pleased with you;
> Keep this in mind as you decide;
> What should you do and what shouldn't you.

Let us pray to Allah to grant us great courage and fortitude, to bless us with complete *Īmān*, unwavering trust and belief in the Holy Qur'ān, and the ability to obey his Commandments as they should be obeyed. May Allah shower *Salāt* and *Salām* in great abundance, on our beloved Prophet (s.a.w.), the best of creation, and upon his family and his Companions.

Doctor Mohammed Ismail Memon
Lailatul Eid-ul-Adha 1410 H
July 3, 1990

GLOSSARY

A.S.	Stands for *Alaihis Salām* meaning, May peace be on him.
ABUL QĀSIM	Another name of Prophet Muhammad (s.a.w.) derived from the name of his son Qasim. Literally, it means the father of Qasim.
ADHĀN	The call for prayers.
AHĀDĪTH	Plural of Hadīth. The sayings of Prophet Muhammad (s.a.w.)
BAI'AH	An oath of allegiance to submit and obey.
BURQA'	A cover-all commonly worn on top of their garments, by Muslim women in Asia, to cover the entire body.
DAYYŪS	One who tolerates indecency and immorality in his wife, or one who does not maintain honour and decency in his wife.
DĪN	Faith. Religion. Life Style.
IHRĀM	Clothes worn by Muslims during the performance of *Hajj*.
FITNAH	Misguidance, Dissuasion from the path led by Allah, Quarrel, destruction, corruption, mischief, rebelliousness, riot, disturbance, and misleading.
GHADD AL-BASAR	Lowering the gaze.

GHAIR-MAHRAM Opposite of *Mahram*, i.e., a man with whom marriage is permissible and, therefore, women must observe *Hijāb* in front of them.

HADĪTH Saying of the Prophet.

HADĪTH QUDSĪ Saying of Allah narrated by the Prophet.

HAJĀMAH The application of a cup shaped instrument to the skin to draw the blood to the surface for bloodletting.

HAJJ Pilgrimage of Muslims to Mecca.

HARĀM A forbidden thing for Muslims by Allah.

HAUDAJ A haudaj (palanquin) was like a little covered room which was mounted on the back of a camel. Women used to travel in it.

HAYĀ Literally, *Hayā* means Shyness. As an Islamic term, *Hayā* implies that shyness which a person feels before his own conscience and before Allah.

HIJĀB *Hijāb* literally means: screen, curtain, partition, and concealment. As a verb, it means to conceal oneself or hide from the view. In Islamic *Sharī'ah*, the word means for a woman to cover, conceal or hide herself from the view of men.

HIJĀB BIL BUYŪT Observing *Hijāb* by staying within home.

HIJRAH The migration of Prophet Muhammad (s.a.w.) from Mecca to Madīnah. This marked the beginning of the Muslim calendar.

IBLĪS	A name of Shaitān (devil)
'IDDAT	Also called *IDDAH*; means the waiting period for a woman before she may remarry after being widowed or divorced.
JĀHILĪYAH	Ignorance.
JALĀBĪB	Plural of *Jalbāb*.
JALBĀB	The outer sheet or coverlet which a woman wraps around her on top of her garments to cover herself from head to toe. It hides her body completely.
JAMA'AH	Congregational prayer.
JIHĀD	Striving in the path of Allah.
KA'BAH	The first house of worship to Allah built in the city of Mecca in Arabian Peninsula by the Prophets Ibrāhīm and his son Ismail (alaihis salam).
MAHĀRIM	Plural of *Mahram*
MAHRAM	A *Mahram* is a man with whom marriage is forbidden and, therefore, women are not required to observe *Hijāb* in front of them. Examples of such men are father, brother, uncle, grandfather, etc.
MAKRŪH	Some thing unpreferable, undesirable, and repulsive.
MASHA-ALLAH	Whatever is Allah's Will. A phrase uttered when one sees good things or good qualities in someone. It implies that all good is by the Will of Allah.

MASJID — The house of worship for Muslims, commonly referred to in English as Mosque.

MASJID-AL-HARĀM — The Masjid (mosque) in Mecca with the Ka'bah in its centre.

MASJID-AL-NABAWĪ — The Masjid (mosque) of the Prophet in Madīnah.

MU'MIN — A faithful Muslim who practices his faith.

MUBĀH — Permissible activities in Islam.

MUBAHĀT — Plural of Mubah.

MUJĀHIDĪN — Those who strive hard in the way of Allah and specially in the battlefields.

MUNAFIQ — A hypocrite.

NAFS — Lower desires for the acquisition of material things and for the satisfaction of sensual appetite.

NIFĀQ — Hypocrisy.

QAS'R — Curtailment of obligatory prayers during journey.

R.A. — Stands for *Radi-Allahu Anhu* or *Radi-Allahu Anha*, which means May Allah be pleased with him or her.

RUKU' — A section containing a number of Verses in Qur'ān.

SALĀM — Peace. Blessings.

SALĀT Benediction for the Holy Prophet. The five times prayers.

SATR The parts of men's and women's bodies which Islamic *Sharī'ah* declared as private parts, and which may not be exposed to others.

SHAITĀN Devil.

SHARA'Ī Legal (according to the Divine Law)

SHARĪ'AH The Islamic Divine Law.

S.A.W. Stands for *Sallallaho Alaihe Wasallam*. A phrase used after the name of the Prophet Muhammad meaning, May Allah's blessings and peace be upon him.

SUNNAH Traditions of the Prophet (s.a.w.)

SŪRAH A chapter in the Holy Qur'ān.

S.W.T. Stands for *Subhānahū Wa Ta'ālā*. A phrase used with the name of Allah meaning, Glorified and Exalted.

TABARRUJ Showing off and exposing one's beauty in order to attract the attention of men.

TABARRUJ AL-JĀHILĪYAH The way women showed off and exposed themselves in the former Days of Ignorance to attract the attention of men.

TAWĀF Circling around the Holy Ka'bah.

TAZKIYAH-I-BĀTIN Purification of *Nafs* and soul.

UMMAH	The followers of Prophet Muhammad (s.a.w.).
UMMUL MO'MINĪN	The mothers of the believers, i.e., the Wives of the Prophet.
WALLĀHU A'LAM	And Allah knows the best.
ZAKĀT	The obligatory charity in Islam.
ZĪNAT	Beauty and grace.
ZINĀ	Adultery. Fornication.

ABOUT THE AUTHOR

Dr. Ismail Memon Madani was born in 1935 in a small town, known as Māngrole, in Jūnāgadh state, India. He was born in a religious family. He was brought up in a religious environment. After the partition of the Indian subcontinent, his family moved to Pakistan and settled in Karachi. Dr. Ismail completed his formal education in Medicine at the Dow Medical College in Karachi in 1961. He also learned Arabic language and other religious subjects in the Darul-Uloom in Karachi.

In 1963 he was appointed the Medical Officer in Saudi Arabia where he stayed till 1986. Half of this time was spent in the holy city of Madinah practising Medicine. However, his practice had become a secondary thing in his life; he spent most of his time in the work of Da'wah. Since his student life, he was involved in the work of Da'wah, and met a number of very pious and well-known scholars of Islam. He has been closely related to Shaikh-ul-Hadīth Maulānā Zakariyā and Shaikh Abul Hassan Alī Nadwī.

In 1986 he migrated to Canada with his family. Three of his four sons have memorized the Holy Qur'ān and have received formal religious education. Two of whom are certified scholars from the Darul-Uloom in Bury, England, and the third and the youngest will receive his diploma next year, Insha-Allah.

After coming to Canada he settled in Ontario and started an Islamic boarding school in the company of Maulana Mazhar Alam in Cornwall where he stayed for 14 months. Then, he moved to Waterloo where his son Maulana Ibrāhīm Memon was appointed the Imam for a local Masjid. In Waterloo, along with his work of Da'wah, he began his quest to establish another Islamic boarding school to train and educate Muslim children in an Islamic environment. After five years of hard work, he succeeded, with the blessing of Almighty Allah, in establishing the Darul-Uloom Al-Madania in Buffalo, New York.

Presently, he resides in Buffalo, New York, with his family. He has given up his practice of Medicine and now keeps himself busy with the affairs of Darul-Uloom and in the work of Da'wah. May Allah give him strength, good health, and a long life to continue with his mission.